Get your facts straight with CGP!

This CGP Knowledge Organiser has one mission in life —
helping you remember the key facts for Edexcel GCSE Biology.

We've boiled every topic down to the vital definitions,
facts and diagrams, making it all easy to memorise.

There's also a matching Knowledge Retriever book that'll test
you on every page. Perfect for making sure you know it all!

CGP — still the best! ☺

Our sole aim here at CGP is to produce the highest quality books —
carefully written, immaculately presented and dangerously close to being funny.

Then we work our socks off to get them out to you
— at the cheapest possible prices.

Contents

Working Scientifically
The Scientific Method..................2
Designing & Performing Experiments..........3
Presenting Data..................4
Conclusions, Evaluations and Units..............5

Topic 1 — Key Concepts in Biology
Cells..................6
Specialised Cells and Enzymes..................7
Enzymes, Energy & Transport in Cells..........8

Topic 2 — Cells and Control
The Cell Cycle..................9
Growth and Stem Cells..................10
The Brain and the Nervous System..............11
Neurones and Reflexes..................12
The Eye..................13

Topic 3 — Genetics
Reproduction..................14
DNA..................15
Protein Synthesis..................16
Inheritance..................17
Genetic Diagrams..................18
Sex-Linked Disorders & Blood Groups...19
Variation & the Human
 Genome Project..................20

Topic 4 — Natural Selection and Genetic Modification
Natural Selection and Evolution..................21
Evidence for Human Evolution..................22
Evidence and Theories of Evolution..............23
Classification and Selective Breeding..........24
Genetic Engineering..................25
World Food Supply & Tissue Culture..............26

Topic 5 — Health, Disease & the Development of Medicines
Health and Disease..................27
Communicable Diseases..................28
STIs and Defences Against Disease..........29
The Immune System..................30
Immunisation and Plant Diseases..................31
Monoclonal Antibodies..................32
Medicines and Lifestyle Factors..................33
Non-Communicable Diseases..................34

Topic 6 — Plant Structures and Their Functions
Photosynthesis..................35
Plant Cells..................36
Transpiration..................37
Adaptations of Leaves and Plants..................38
Plant Hormones..................39

Topic 7 — Animal Coordination, Control & Homeostasis

Hormones...40
The Menstrual Cycle.............................41
Controlling Fertility..............................42
Homeostasis — Blood Glucose...........43
Thermoregulation & Osmoregulation....44
The Kidneys..45

Topic 8 — Exchange and Transport in Animals

Exchange of Materials..........................46
Blood and Blood Vessels......................47
The Heart and Respiration..................48

Topic 9 — Ecosystems and Material Cycles

Ecosystems and Organism Interactions....49
Biomass and Energy Transfers............50
Human Impacts on Biodiversity..........51
Food Security..52
Cycling of Materials.............................53
Nitrogen...54
Indicator Species and Decomposition....55

Core Practicals

Core Practicals 1..................................56
Core Practicals 2..................................57
Core Practicals 3..................................58
Core Practicals 4..................................59
Core Practicals 5..................................60

Practical Skills

Practical Techniques.............................61
Measurements......................................62

Published by CGP.
From original material by Richard Parsons.

Editors: Ellen Burton, Sarah Pattison, Claire Plowman, Rachael Rogers.
Contributor: Paddy Gannon.

With thanks to Susan Alexander and Emily Forsberg for the proofreading.
With thanks to Emily Smith for the copyright research.

ISBN: 978 1 78908 849 6

Percentile growth chart on p.10 copyright © 2009 Royal College of Paediatrics and Child Health.

Definition of health on p.27 reproduced from the Preamble to the Constitution of the World Health Organization as adopted by the International Health Conference, New York, 19 June - 22 July 1946; signed on 22 July 1946 by the representatives of 61 States (Official Records of the World Health Organization, no. 2, p.100) and entered into force on 7 April 1948.

Printed by Elanders Ltd, Newcastle upon Tyne.
Clipart from Corel®
Illustrations by: Sandy Gardner Artist, email sandy@sandygardner.co.uk

Text, design, layout and original illustrations © Coordination Group Publications Ltd (CGP) 2022
All rights reserved.

Photocopying more than one section of this book is not permitted, even if you have a CLA licence.
Extra copies are available from CGP with next day delivery. • 0800 1712 712 • www.cgpbooks.co.uk

The Scientific Method

Developing Theories

Come up with hypothesis
↓
Test hypothesis
↓
Evidence is peer-reviewed
↓
If all evidence backs up hypothesis, it becomes an accepted theory.

HYPOTHESIS — a possible explanation for an observation.

PEER REVIEW — when other scientists check results and explanations before they're published.

Accepted theories can still change over time as more evidence is found, e.g. inheritance and genetics:

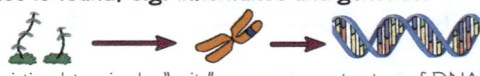

characteristics determined by "hereditary units" → "units" are genes on chromosomes → structure of DNA shows how genes work

Models

REPRESENTATIONAL MODELS — a simplified description or picture of the real system, e.g. lock and key model of enzyme action:

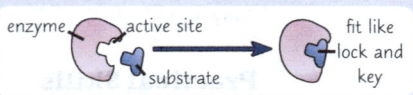

enzyme, active site, substrate → fit like lock and key

Models help scientists explain observations and make predictions.

COMPUTATIONAL MODELS — computers are used to simulate complex processes.

Issues in Science

Scientific developments can create four types of issue:

1. **Economic** — e.g. beneficial technology, like alternative energy sources, may be too expensive to use.
2. **Environmental** — e.g. new technology could harm the natural environment.
3. **Social** — decisions based on research can affect society, e.g. taxing alcohol to reduce health problems.
4. **Personal** — some decisions affect individuals, e.g. a person may not want a wind farm being built near to their home.

Media reports on scientific developments may be oversimplified, inaccurate or biased.

Hazard and Risk

HAZARD — something that could potentially cause harm.

RISK — the chance that a hazard will cause harm.

Hazards associated with biology experiments include:

- Some microorganisms can make you ill.
- Hazardous chemicals (e.g. flammable ethanol).
- Faulty electrical equipment can give you a shock.

The seriousness of the harm and the likelihood of it happening both need consideration.

Designing & Performing Experiments

Collecting Data

Data should be...	
REPEATABLE	Same person gets same results after repeating experiment using the same method and equipment.
REPRODUCIBLE	Similar results can be achieved by someone else, or by using a different method or piece of equipment.
ACCURATE	Results are close to the true answer.
PRECISE	All data is close to the mean.

Reliable data is repeatable and reproducible.

Valid results are repeatable and reproducible and answer the original question.

Fair Tests

INDEPENDENT VARIABLE	Variable that you change.
DEPENDENT VARIABLE	Variable that is measured.
CONTROL VARIABLE	Variable that is kept the same.
CONTROL EXPERIMENT	An experiment kept under the same conditions as the rest of the investigation without anything being done to it.
FAIR TEST	An experiment where only the independent variable changes, whilst all other variables are kept the same.

An "indie" variable

Control experiments are carried out when variables can't be controlled.

Four Things to Look Out For

1. **RANDOM ERRORS** — unpredictable differences caused by things like human errors in measuring.
2. **SYSTEMATIC ERRORS** — measurements that are wrong by the same amount each time.
3. **ZERO ERRORS** — systematic errors that are caused by using a piece of equipment that isn't zeroed properly.
4. **ANOMALOUS RESULTS** — results that don't fit with the rest of the data.

Anomalous results can be ignored if you know what caused them.

Processing Data

Calculate the **mean** — add together all repeat measurements and divide by number of measurements.

UNCERTAINTY — the amount by which a mean result may differ from the true value.

$$\text{uncertainty} = \frac{\text{range}}{2}$$

largest measurement minus smallest measurement

In any calculation, you should round the answer to the lowest number of significant figures (s.f.) given.

Working Scientifically

Presenting Data

Bar Charts

Bar charts are used when independent variable is categoric or discrete.

- linear scale
- units
- labelled axes
- Key — used when there are multiple data sets.
- gaps between categories

Discrete data can only take certain values with no in-between values.

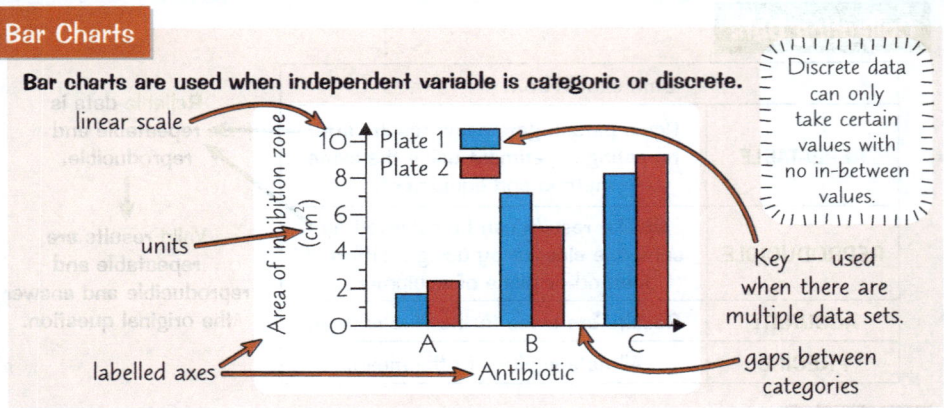

(Bar chart: Area of inhibition zone (cm^2) vs Antibiotic A, B, C, showing Plate 1 and Plate 2)

Plotting Graphs

Graphs can be used when both variables are continuous.

Continuous data — can take any numerical value within a range.

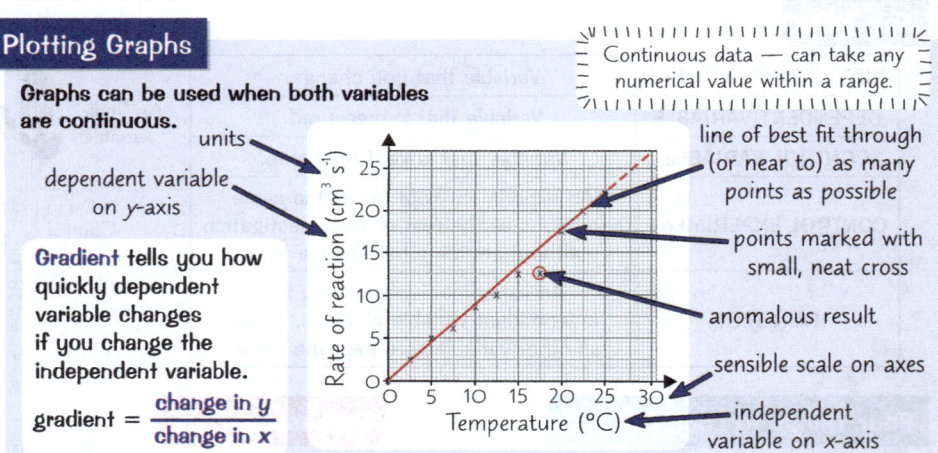

- units
- dependent variable on y-axis
- line of best fit through (or near to) as many points as possible
- points marked with small, neat cross
- anomalous result
- sensible scale on axes
- independent variable on x-axis

Gradient tells you how quickly dependent variable changes if you change the independent variable.

$$\text{gradient} = \frac{\text{change in } y}{\text{change in } x}$$

(Graph: Rate of reaction ($cm^3 \, s^{-1}$) vs Temperature (°C))

Three Types of Correlation Between Variables

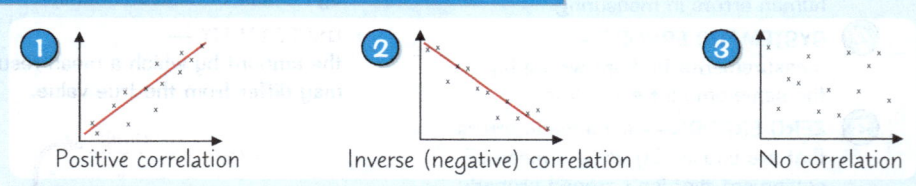

1. Positive correlation
2. Inverse (negative) correlation
3. No correlation

Possible reasons for a correlation:

Chance — correlation might be a fluke.

Third variable — another factor links the two variables.

Cause — if every other variable that could affect the result is controlled, you can conclude that changing one variable causes the change in the other.

Working Scientifically

Conclusions, Evaluations and Units

Conclusions

Draw conclusion by stating relationship between dependent and independent variables.

↓

Justify conclusion using specific data.

↓

Refer to original hypothesis and state whether data supports it.

You can only draw a conclusion from what your data shows — you can't go any further than that.

Evaluations

EVALUATION — a critical analysis of the whole investigation.

	Things to consider
Method	• Validity of method • Control of variables
Results	• Reliability, accuracy, precision and reproducibility of results • Number of measurements taken • Level of uncertainty in the results
Anomalous results	• Causes of any anomalous results

Repeating experiment with changes to improve the quality of results will give you more confidence in your conclusions.

You could make more predictions based on your conclusion, which you could test in future experiments.

S.I. Units

S.I. BASE UNITS — a set of standard units that all scientists use.

Quantity	S.I. Unit
mass	kilogram (kg)
length	metre (m)
time	second (s)

Scaling Units

SCALING PREFIX — a word or symbol that goes before a unit to indicate a multiplying factor.

Multiple of unit	Prefix
10^{12}	tera (T)
10^{9}	giga (G)
10^{6}	mega (M)
1000	kilo (k)
0.1	deci (d)
0.01	centi (c)
0.001	milli (m)
10^{-6}	micro (μ)
10^{-9}	nano (n)
10^{-12}	pico (p)

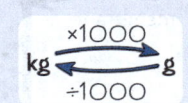

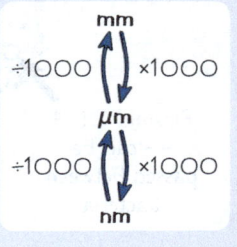

kg ×1000 / ÷1000 g

mm ÷1000 / ×1000 μm ÷1000 / ×1000 nm

Working Scientifically

Cells

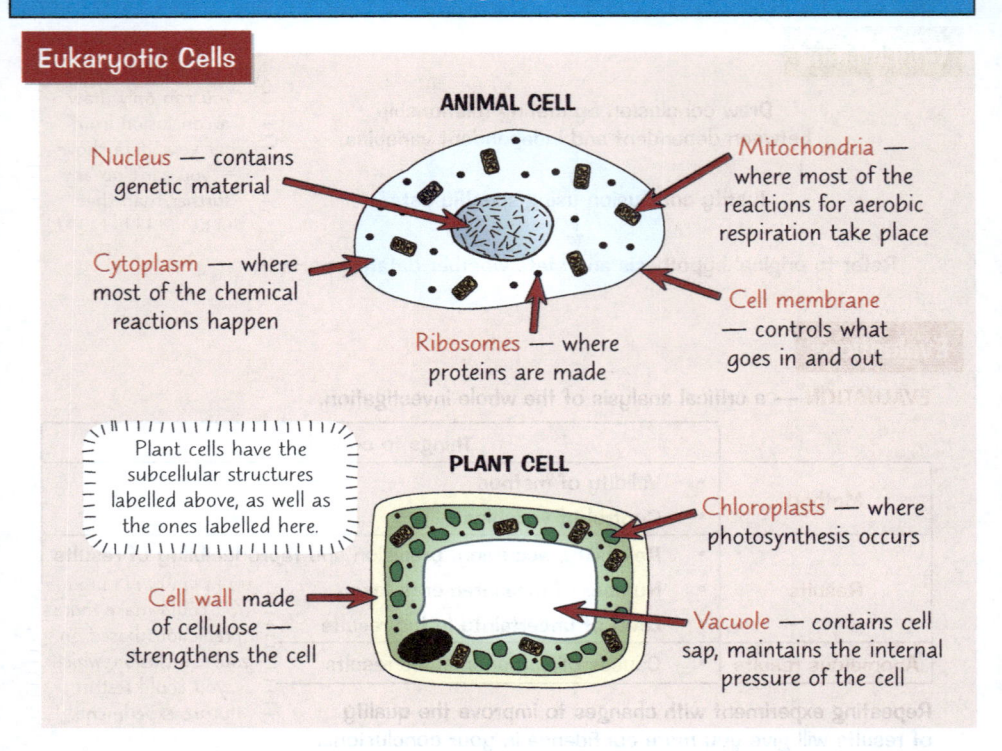

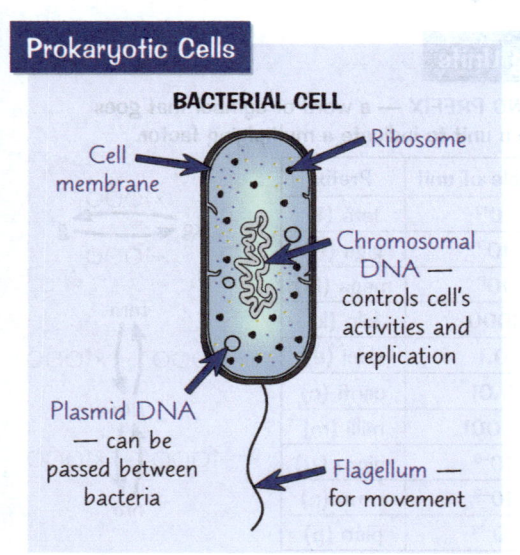

Eukaryotic Cells

ANIMAL CELL

- Nucleus — contains genetic material
- Mitochondria — where most of the reactions for aerobic respiration take place
- Cytoplasm — where most of the chemical reactions happen
- Ribosomes — where proteins are made
- Cell membrane — controls what goes in and out

Plant cells have the subcellular structures labelled above, as well as the ones labelled here.

PLANT CELL

- Chloroplasts — where photosynthesis occurs
- Cell wall made of cellulose — strengthens the cell
- Vacuole — contains cell sap, maintains the internal pressure of the cell

Prokaryotic Cells

BACTERIAL CELL

- Cell membrane
- Ribosome
- Chromosomal DNA — controls cell's activities and replication
- Plasmid DNA — can be passed between bacteria
- Flagellum — for movement

Microscopy

Electron microscopes were invented later than light microscopes.

They have a higher magnification and resolution than light microscopes.

This means they let us see smaller things in more detail, so we can understand subcellular structures better now.

Specialised Cells and Enzymes

Three Specialised Cells

SPECIALISED CELL — a cell that has a structure adapted to its function.

1. Egg cell — carries female DNA and feeds developing embryo
- nutrients in cytoplasm
- haploid nucleus
- cell membrane changes structure after fertilisation to prevent more sperm entering

Haploid nuclei contain half the chromosomes of a normal body cell. When an egg and sperm cell join, they make a cell with the normal number of chromosomes.

2. Sperm cell — transports male DNA to egg
- haploid nucleus
- acrosome contains enzymes for digesting egg membrane
- tail for swimming to egg
- lots of mitochondria to provide energy for swimming

3. Ciliated epithelial cell — moves substances along internal surfaces (e.g. mucus in airways)
- cilia 'beat' to move substances

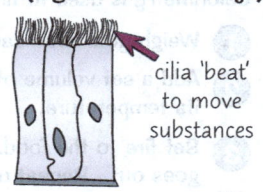

Enzymes

Enzymes catalyse (speed up) chemical reactions.

Each enzyme only catalyses one specific reaction because of the unique shape of its **active site**.

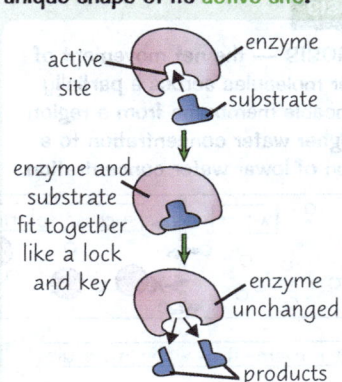

- active site
- enzyme
- substrate
- enzyme and substrate fit together like a lock and key
- enzyme unchanged
- products

Factors Affecting Enzyme Activity

High temperatures and high and low pHs **denature** enzymes (change the shape of the active site so the enzyme no longer works).

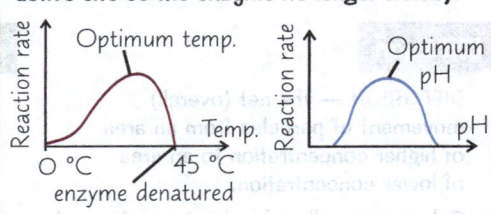

Reaction rate vs Temp.: Optimum temp., 0 °C, 45 °C enzyme denatured

Reaction rate vs pH: Optimum pH

More substrate molecules means enzyme and substrate are more likely to meet.

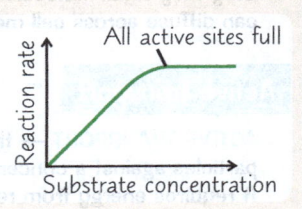

Reaction rate vs Substrate concentration: All active sites full

Topic 1 — Key Concepts in Biology

Enzymes, Energy & Transport in Cells

Enzymes in Organisms

Enzymes break big molecules into smaller ones, which are used for life processes.

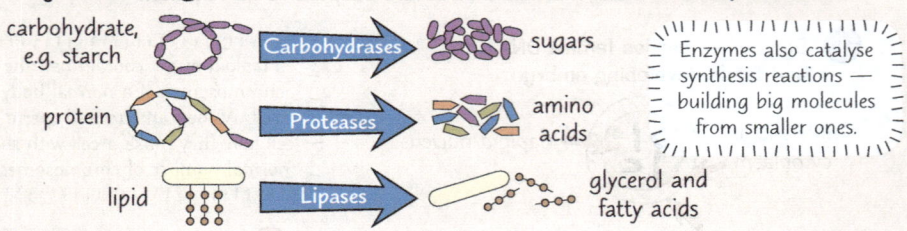

- carbohydrate, e.g. starch → **Carbohydrases** → sugars
- protein → **Proteases** → amino acids
- lipid → **Lipases** → glycerol and fatty acids

Enzymes also catalyse synthesis reactions — building big molecules from smaller ones.

Energy in Food

Calorimetry is used to find the amount of energy in food.

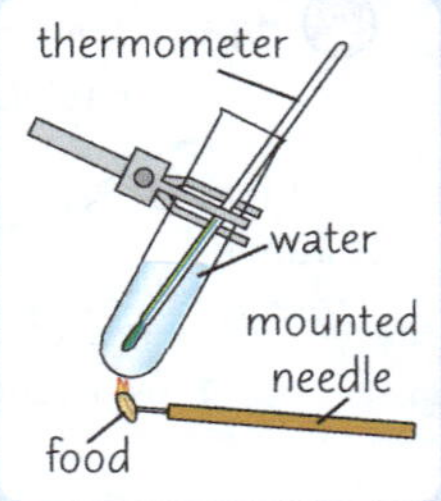

1. Weigh your food sample then put it on a mounted needle.
2. Add a set volume of water to a boiling tube and record its temperature.
3. Set fire to the food. Hold it under the boiling tube until it goes out. Repeat until the food no longer catches fire.
4. Record the temperature of the water.

Find the energy per gram of food:

1 cm^3 of water = 1 g of water

Energy in food (J) = mass of water (g) × temperature change of water (°C) × **4.2**

Energy per gram of food (J/g) = energy in food (J) ÷ mass of food (g)

Diffusion

DIFFUSION — the net (overall) movement of particles from an area of higher concentration to an area of lower concentration.

Only very small molecules (e.g. glucose) can diffuse across cell membranes.

Active Transport

ACTIVE TRANSPORT — the movement of particles against a concentration gradient. It requires energy from respiration.

Osmosis

OSMOSIS — the net movement of water molecules across a partially permeable membrane from a region of higher water concentration to a region of lower water concentration.

Topic 1 — Key Concepts in Biology

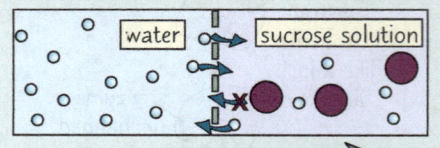

Topic 2 — Cells and Control

The Cell Cycle

Chromosomes and the Cell Cycle

CHROMOSOMES — coiled up lengths of DNA molecules, which carry genes. They're found in the nucleus and they're normally in pairs in body cells.

Cells with two copies of each chromosome are 'diploid'.

CELL CYCLE — a series of stages in which cells divide to produce new cells.

When a cell is not dividing, it is in interphase.
Before dividing, it does three things:

1. Grows in size.
2. Increases the amount of subcellular structures, e.g. mitochondria and ribosomes.
3. Duplicates its DNA.

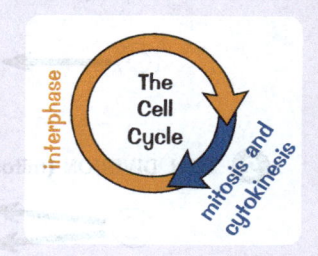

The Cell Cycle: interphase → mitosis and cytokinesis

Mitosis is okay, but check out my toesies.

Mitosis

MITOSIS — the stage of the cell cycle when the cell divides.

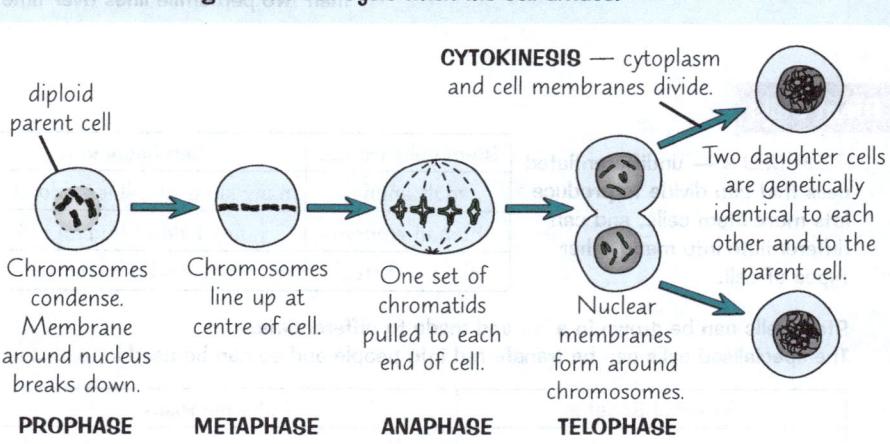

CYTOKINESIS — cytoplasm and cell membranes divide.

- diploid parent cell
- Chromosomes condense. Membrane around nucleus breaks down. — **PROPHASE**
- Chromosomes line up at centre of cell. — **METAPHASE**
- One set of chromatids pulled to each end of cell. — **ANAPHASE**
- Nuclear membranes form around chromosomes. — **TELOPHASE**
- Two daughter cells are genetically identical to each other and to the parent cell.

Mitosis allows organisms to grow or replace cells that have been damaged. Some organisms use mitosis in asexual reproduction.

If there's a change in one of the genes that controls cell division, the cell may start dividing uncontrollably. This can result in cancer.

Growth and Stem Cells

Three Methods of Growth

Plants and animals grow due to:

1. **CELL DIFFERENTIATION** — the process by which a cell changes to become specialised for its job.

2. **CELL DIVISION** (mitosis)

3. **CELL ELONGATION** (plants only)

Percentile Charts

Percentile charts are used to monitor a child's growth.

Mass, length and head circumference are monitored over time.

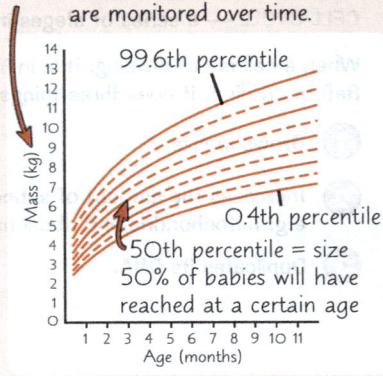

- 99.6th percentile
- 0.4th percentile
- 50th percentile = size 50% of babies will have reached at a certain age

Doctors may be concerned if, e.g. a baby's size was below the 0.4th percentile or changed by more than two percentile lines over time.

Stem Cells

STEM CELLS — undifferentiated cells that can divide to produce lots more stem cells, and can differentiate into many other types of cell.

Stem cells from...	Can become...
adult animal	many kinds of cell, e.g. blood cells
human embryo	any kind of human cell
plant meristem	any kind of plant cell

Stem cells can be grown in a lab and made to differentiate.
The specialised cells can be transferred into people and so can be used in medicine:

Potential Benefits	Potential Risks
• Could replace cells that have been damaged by disease or injury, e.g. new cardiac muscle cells could treat heart disease.	• Tumour development. • Disease transmission (if donor stem cells are infected with a virus). • Rejection by patient's immune system.

Topic 2 — Cells and Control

The Brain and the Nervous System

The Brain

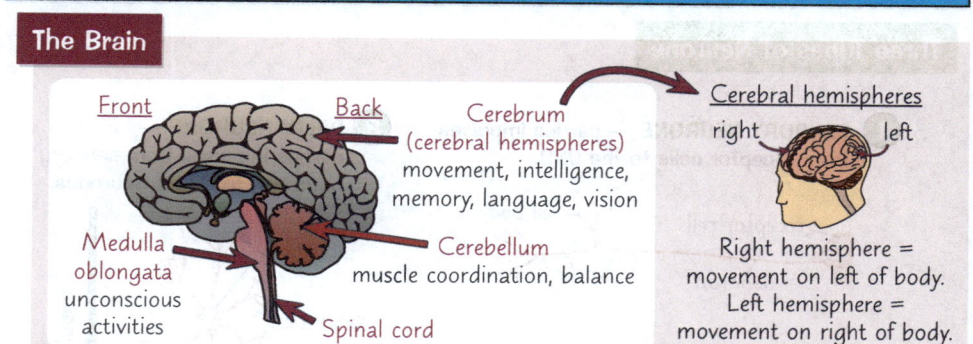

Cerebrum (cerebral hemispheres) — movement, intelligence, memory, language, vision

Medulla oblongata — unconscious activities

Cerebellum — muscle coordination, balance

Spinal cord

Cerebral hemispheres
Right hemisphere = movement on left of body.
Left hemisphere = movement on right of body.

CENTRAL NERVOUS SYSTEM (CNS) — consists of the brain and spinal cord.

The CNS is complex and delicate, so investigating or treating it is difficult. E.g.:
- tumours can grow in parts of the brain that are hard to access,
- operating on the brain or spinal cord risks permanent damage,
- CNS nervous tissue can't be repaired.

Two methods for studying the brain without surgery:

1. **CT scanning** — X-ray image shows the main structures of the brain.
2. **PET scanning** — radioactive chemicals show which parts of the brain are active.

The Nervous System

NEURONES — cells that carry information as electrical impulses in the nervous system. The nervous system means that humans can react to their surroundings and coordinate their behaviour.

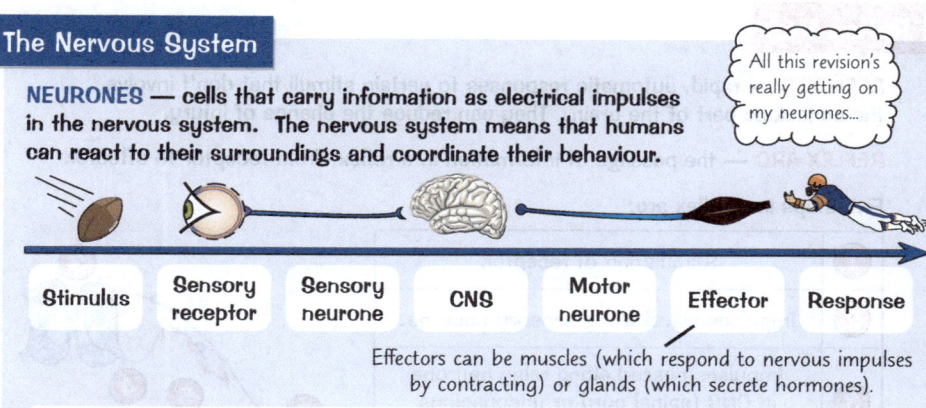

All this revision's really getting on my neurones...

Stimulus → Sensory receptor → Sensory neurone → CNS → Motor neurone → Effector → Response

Effectors can be muscles (which respond to nervous impulses by contracting) or glands (which secrete hormones).

SYNAPSE — the connection between two neurones. A nerve signal is transferred across a synapse by the diffusion of **neurotransmitters**.

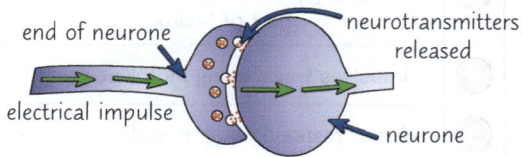

end of neurone → electrical impulse → neurotransmitters released → neurone

Topic 2 — Cells and Control

Neurones and Reflexes

Three Types of Neurone

1) SENSORY NEURONE — carries impulses from receptor cells to the CNS.

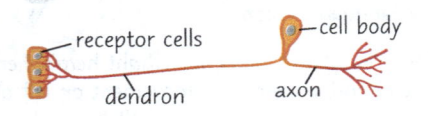

- receptor cells
- cell body
- dendron
- axon

2) MOTOR NEURONE — carries impulses from the CNS to effector cells.

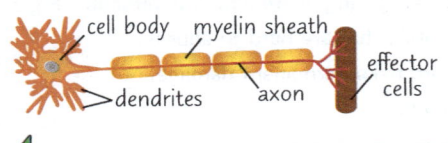

- cell body
- myelin sheath
- dendrites
- axon
- effector cells

← Not all motor neurones have myelin sheaths. Sensory and relay neurones can be myelinated too.

3) RELAY NEURONE — carries impulses from sensory neurones to motor neurones.

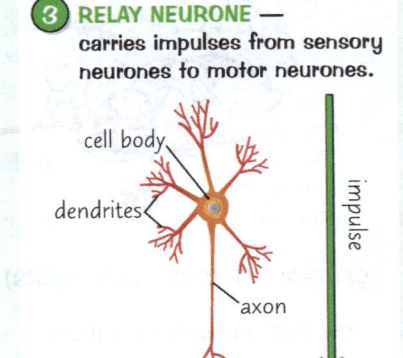

- cell body
- dendrites
- axon
- impulse

The myelin sheath acts as an insulator, speeding up the electrical impulse.

Reflex Arcs

REFLEXES — rapid, automatic responses to certain stimuli that don't involve the conscious part of the brain. They can reduce the chance of injury.

REFLEX ARC — the passage of information in a reflex, from receptor to effector.

Five steps in a reflex arc:

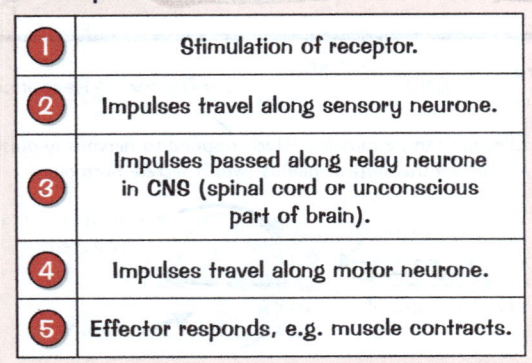

1	Stimulation of receptor.
2	Impulses travel along sensory neurone.
3	Impulses passed along relay neurone in CNS (spinal cord or unconscious part of brain).
4	Impulses travel along motor neurone.
5	Effector responds, e.g. muscle contracts.

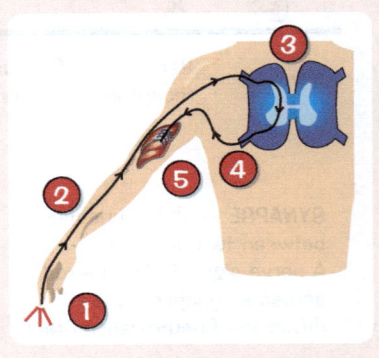

Topic 2 — Cells and Control

The Eye

Structure of the Eye

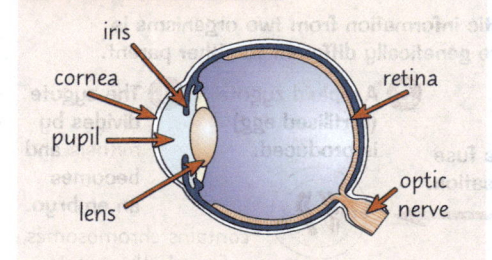

Labels: iris, cornea, pupil, lens, retina, optic nerve

Lens	Focuses light onto retina.
Cornea	Refracts (bends) light into eye.
Iris	Contains muscles controlling pupil size.
Retina	Contains receptor cells sensitive to light intensity (rods) and colour (cones).
Optic nerve	Carries impulses from receptor cells to brain.

Focusing the Eye

To look at near objects:
- near object
- lens becomes thicker
- light refracted more

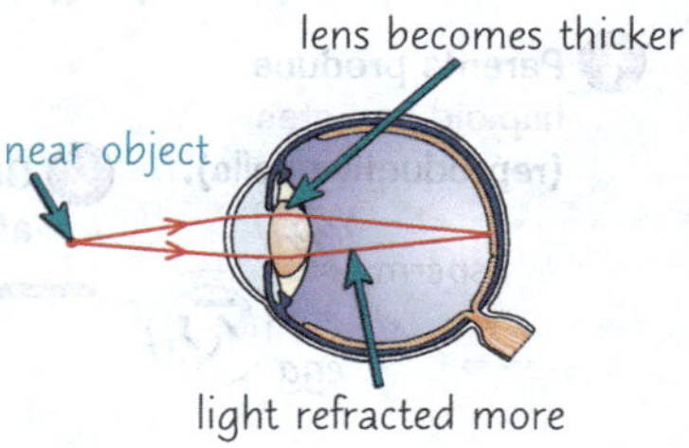

To look at distant objects:
- distant object
- lens becomes thinner
- light refracted less

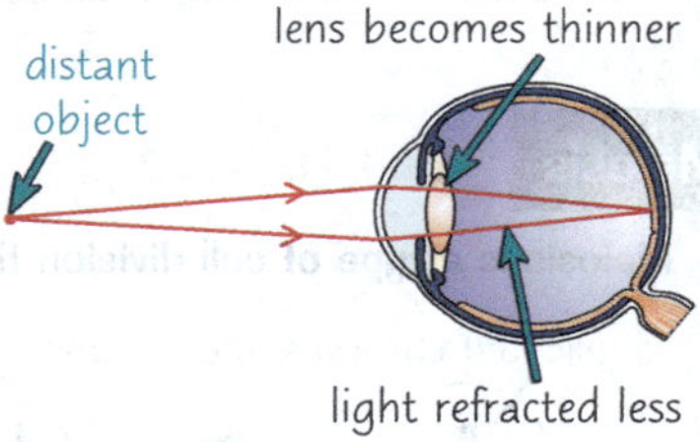

Four Common Defects of the Eye

1. Long-sightedness: lens doesn't bend light enough or eyeball too short
- Image of near objects brought into focus behind retina.
- Fixed using convex lens.

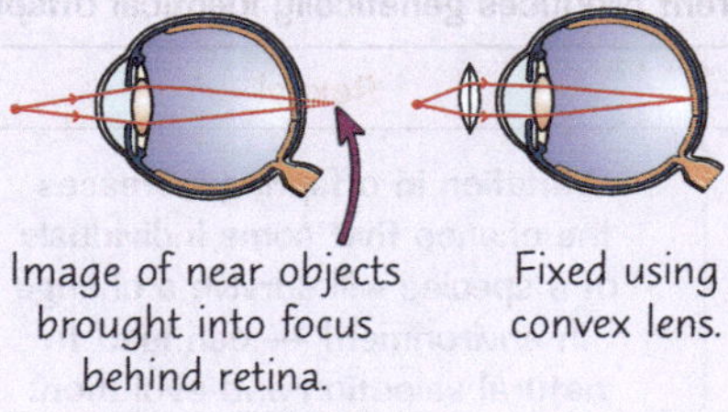

2. Short-sightedness: lens bends light too much or eyeball too long
- Image of distant objects brought into focus in front of retina.
- Fixed using concave lens.

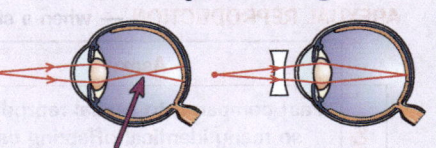

3. Colour blindness: Some cones don't work properly so colours are hard to tell apart.

4. Cataracts: Cloudy patch on the lens — causes blurred vision. Fixed by replacing lens with an artificial one.

Topic 2 — Cells and Control

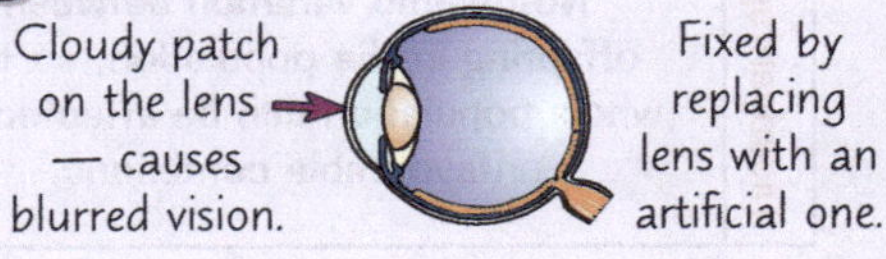

Reproduction

Sexual Reproduction

SEXUAL REPRODUCTION — when genetic information from two organisms is combined to produce offspring which are genetically different to either parent.

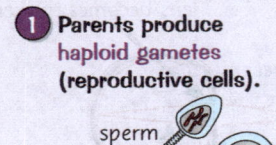

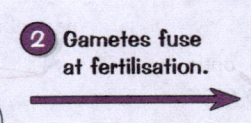

1. Parents produce **haploid gametes** (reproductive cells).
2. Gametes fuse at fertilisation.
3. A **diploid zygote** (fertilised egg) is produced.
4. The zygote divides by **mitosis** and becomes an embryo.

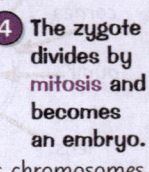

sperm + egg → contains chromosomes from both parents

CHROMOSOMES — long molecules of DNA that normally come in pairs.
HAPLOID — containing **half** the number of chromosomes of normal cells.
DIPLOID — containing a **full** set of chromosomes.

Normal cells are diploid.

Meiosis

Meiosis is a type of cell division that produces **four haploid** daughter cells.

duplicated chromosomes → division 1 → one copy of each chromosome → division 2 → haploid gametes

All the gametes produced by meiosis are genetically different.

Reproduction Pros and Cons

Cells divide by mitosis.

ASEXUAL REPRODUCTION — when a single parent produces genetically identical offspring.

	Asexual	Sexual
Advantages	Fast compared to sexual reproduction, so many identical offspring can be produced in favourable conditions. Only one parent needed, so no energy wasted finding a mate.	Variation in offspring increases the chance that some individuals of a species will survive a change in environment — can lead to natural selection and evolution.
Disadvantages	No genetic variation between offspring in the population, so the whole population can be affected by unfavourable conditions.	Need to find a mate, which takes time and energy. Hard for isolated individuals.

DNA

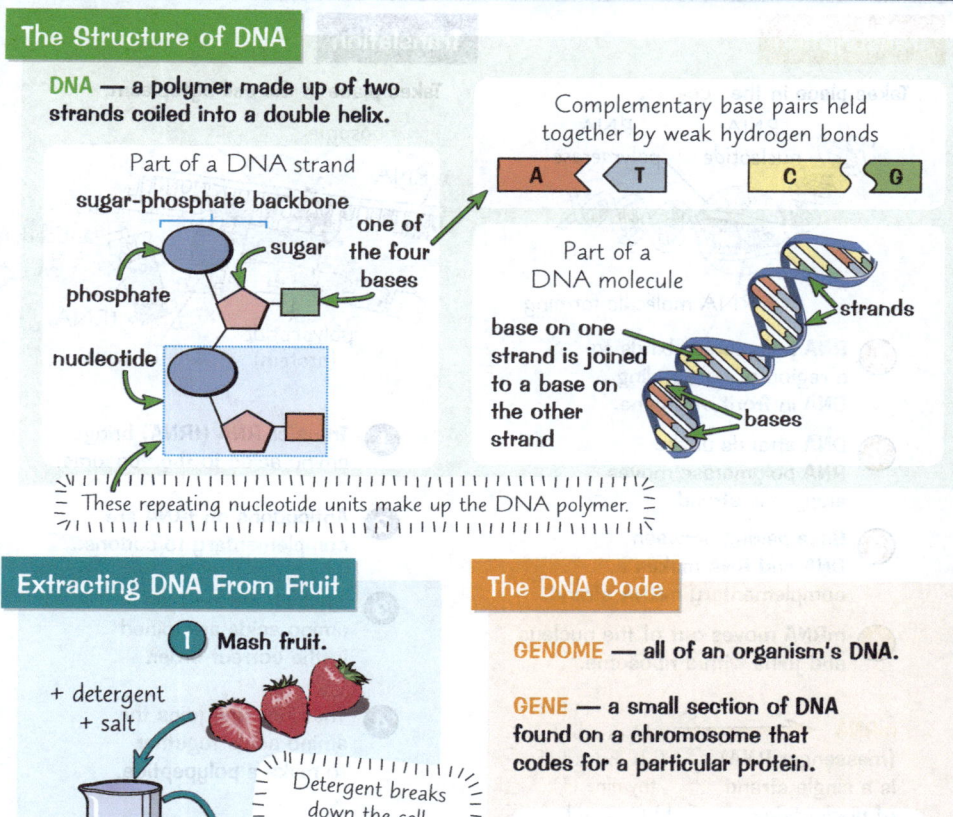

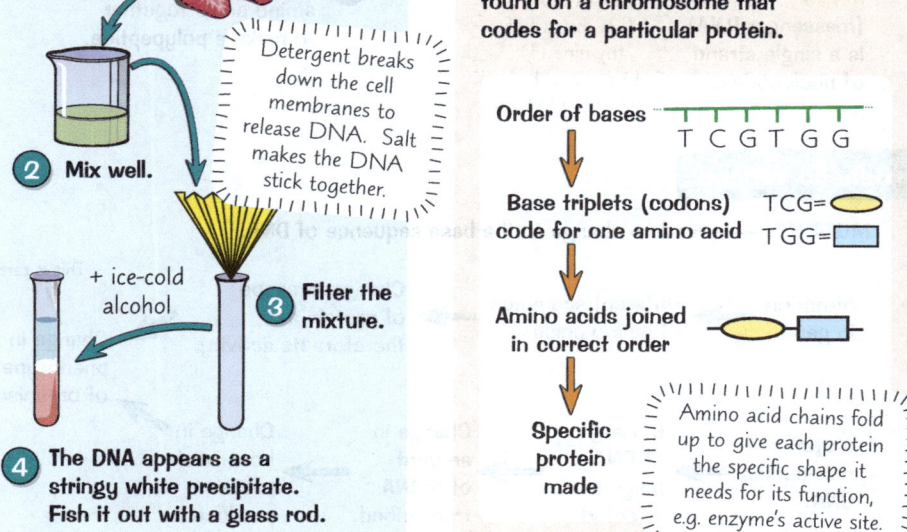

The Structure of DNA

DNA — a polymer made up of two strands coiled into a double helix.

Part of a DNA strand
- sugar-phosphate backbone
- sugar
- one of the four bases
- phosphate
- nucleotide

Complementary base pairs held together by weak hydrogen bonds

A — T   C — G

Part of a DNA molecule
- strands
- base on one strand is joined to a base on the other strand
- bases

These repeating nucleotide units make up the DNA polymer.

Extracting DNA From Fruit

1. **Mash fruit.**
   + detergent
   + salt

2. **Mix well.**

Detergent breaks down the cell membranes to release DNA. Salt makes the DNA stick together.

3. **Filter the mixture.**
   + ice-cold alcohol

4. **The DNA appears as a stringy white precipitate. Fish it out with a glass rod.**

The DNA Code

GENOME — all of an organism's DNA.

GENE — a small section of DNA found on a chromosome that codes for a particular protein.

Order of bases: T C G T G G

↓

Base triplets (codons) code for one amino acid
TCG = ◯
TGG = ▭

↓

Amino acids joined in correct order

↓

Specific protein made

Amino acid chains fold up to give each protein the specific shape it needs for its function, e.g. enzyme's active site.

Topic 3 — Genetics

Protein Synthesis

Transcription

Takes place in the nucleus.

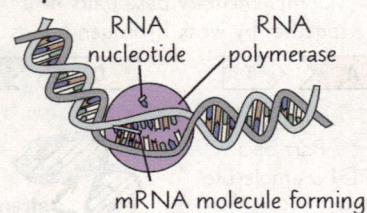

mRNA molecule forming, with RNA nucleotide and RNA polymerase labelled.

1. RNA polymerase binds to a region of non-coding DNA in front of a gene.
2. DNA strands unzip. RNA polymerase moves along one strand.
3. Base pairing between DNA and RNA makes a complementary mRNA strand.
4. mRNA moves out of the nucleus and joins with a ribosome.

mRNA (messenger RNA) is a single strand of nucleotides. — Uses uracil (U) instead of thymine (T). U pairs with A.

Translation

Takes place in the cell cytoplasm.

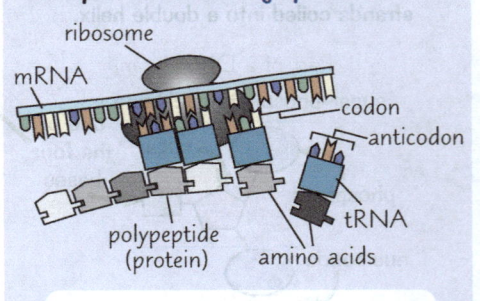

Ribosome on mRNA, with codon, anticodon, tRNA, amino acids, and polypeptide (protein) labelled.

1. Transfer RNA (tRNA) brings amino acids to the ribosome.
2. Anticodons on tRNA are complementary to codons...
3. ...which means the amino acids are joined in the correct order.
4. The ribosome joins the amino acids together to make a polypeptide.

Genetic Variants

MUTATION — a random change to the base sequence of DNA.

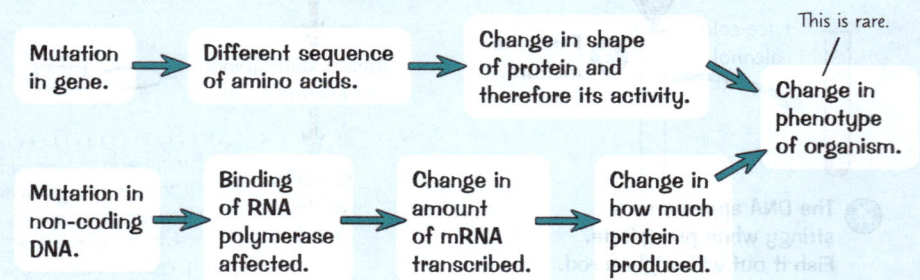

Mutation in gene. → Different sequence of amino acids. → Change in shape of protein and therefore its activity. → Change in phenotype of organism. *(This is rare.)*

Mutation in non-coding DNA. → Binding of RNA polymerase affected. → Change in amount of mRNA transcribed. → Change in how much protein produced. → Change in phenotype of organism.

Inheritance

The Work of Mendel

Mendel studied how characteristics in plants were passed on from one generation to the next.

The results of his research were published in 1866 and became the foundation of modern genetics.

Scientists of Mendel's day didn't have the background to properly understand his findings but after he died they:

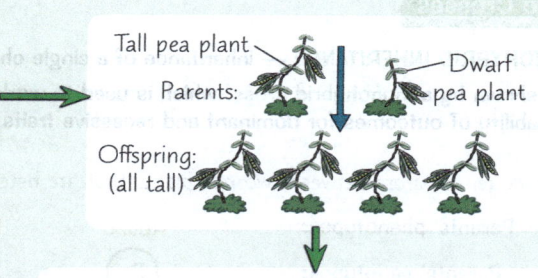

Parents: Tall pea plant — Dwarf pea plant
Offspring: (all tall)

Three of Mendel's Conclusions

1. 'Hereditary units' determine characteristics.
2. The units are passed on to offspring unchanged.
3. The units can be dominant or recessive.

- learnt about chromosomes
- proposed Mendel's 'units' = genes
- determined the structure of DNA

Told ya

Genetic Terms

ALLELE	A version of a gene.
DOMINANT	An allele that is always expressed.
RECESSIVE	An allele that is only expressed when two copies are present.
HOMOZYGOUS	Both of an organism's alleles for a trait are the same.
HETEROZYGOUS	An organism's alleles for a trait are different.
GENOTYPE	An organism's combination of alleles.
PHENOTYPE	The characteristics an organism has.

- Some characteristics are controlled by a single gene but most are controlled by multiple genes.
- Body cells have two alleles of every gene — one on each chromosome.

Topic 3 — Genetics

Genetic Diagrams

Genetic Crosses

MONOHYBRID INHERITANCE — inheritance of a single characteristic.
It is shown by a monohybrid cross, which is used to work out the probability of outcomes for dominant and recessive traits.

A genetic cross between two pea plants that are heterozygous for pea type.

Parents' phenotypes:	Round Round	r = recessive allele for wrinkly peas
Parents' genotypes:	Rr Rr	
Gametes' genotypes:	R r R r	
Offspring's genotypes:	RR Rr Rr rr	
Offspring's phenotypes:	Round Round Round Wrinkly	

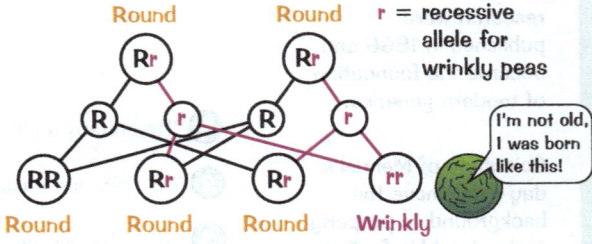

I'm not old, I was born like this!

That's a **3:1 ratio** of round to wrinkly offspring.

Sex Determination

Human body cells have 23 pairs of chromosomes.
The 23rd pair determines sex.

A Punnett square for X and Y chromosome sex determination.

Gametes' genotypes

female gametes: X X
male gametes: X, Y

	X	X
X	XX female	XX female
Y	XY male	XY male

Offspring's genotypes

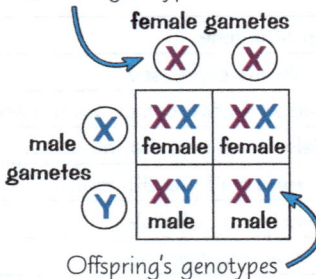

That's a **1:1 ratio** of male to female offspring.

Family Pedigrees

Horizontal lines link parents.
Vertical lines connect parents to children.

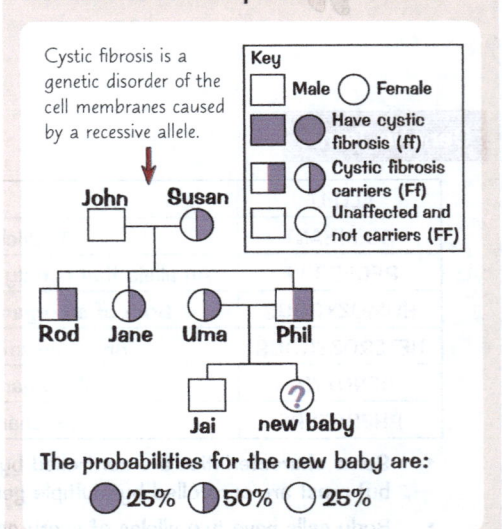

Cystic fibrosis is a genetic disorder of the cell membranes caused by a recessive allele.

Key:
- ☐ Male ◯ Female
- Have cystic fibrosis (ff)
- Cystic fibrosis carriers (Ff)
- Unaffected and not carriers (FF)

Pedigree: John — Susan → children: Rod, Jane, Uma, Phil → Phil's children: Jai, new baby (?)

The probabilities for the new baby are:
● 25%   ◐ 50%   ◯ 25%

Topic 3 — Genetics

Sex-Linked Disorders & Blood Groups

Sex-linked Disorders

SEX-LINKED DISORDER — when the allele that codes for a disorder is located on a sex chromosome (X or Y).

Most genes on sex chromosomes are only carried on the X chromosome (much bigger than Y). Men only have one copy of lots of sex-linked genes, so are likely to show the characteristic even if allele they have is recessive.

Male sex chromosomes
- X chromosome — just one allele for this gene
- Y chromosome
- two alleles for this gene

Colour-blindness is a sex-linked disorder:

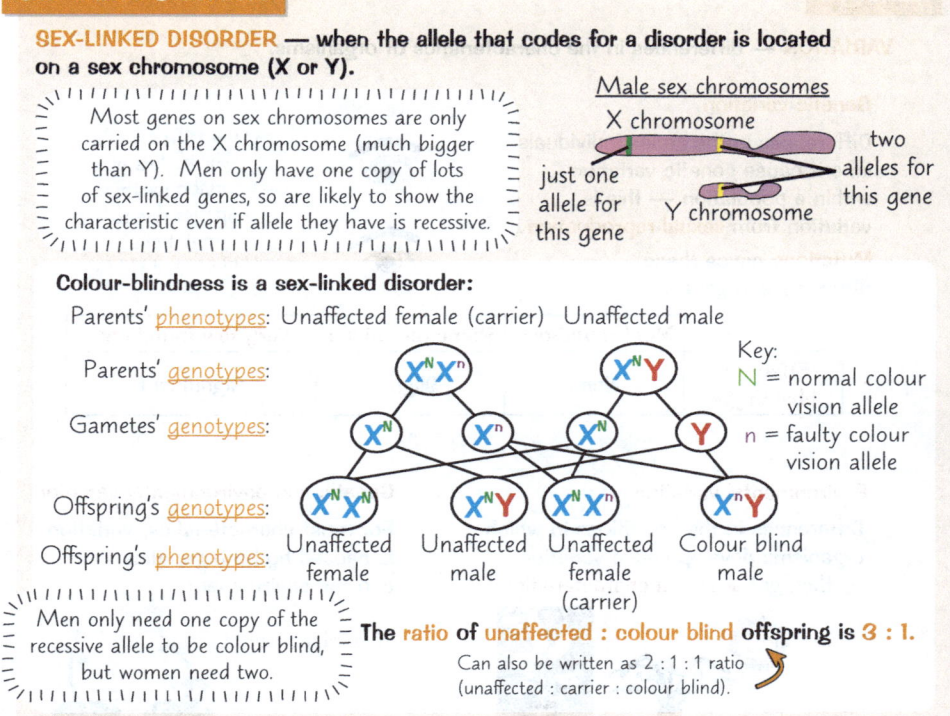

Parents' _phenotypes_: Unaffected female (carrier)   Unaffected male

Parents' _genotypes_: $X^N X^n$ $X^N Y$

Gametes' _genotypes_: X^N, X^n, X^N, Y

Offspring's _genotypes_: $X^N X^N$, $X^N Y$, $X^N X^n$, $X^n Y$

Offspring's _phenotypes_: Unaffected female, Unaffected male, Unaffected female (carrier), Colour blind male

Key:
N = normal colour vision allele
n = faulty colour vision allele

Men only need one copy of the recessive allele to be colour blind, but women need two.

The **ratio** of **unaffected : colour blind** offspring is **3 : 1**.
Can also be written as 2 : 1 : 1 ratio (unaffected : carrier : colour blind).

Blood Groups

- There are three different alleles for blood type — I^O, I^A and I^B.
- I^A and I^B are **codominant**. I^O is **recessive**.
- There are four blood groups — O, A, B and AB.

CODOMINANT — one allele isn't dominant over the other.

E.g:
Parents' phenotypes: Heterozygous Blood group A   Heterozygous Blood group B

Parents' genotypes: $I^A I^O$ $I^B I^O$

Gametes' alleles: I^A, I^O, I^B, I^O

Possible offspring:
- $I^A I^B$ — Group AB
- $I^A I^O$ — Group A
- $I^B I^O$ — Group B
- $I^O I^O$ — Group O

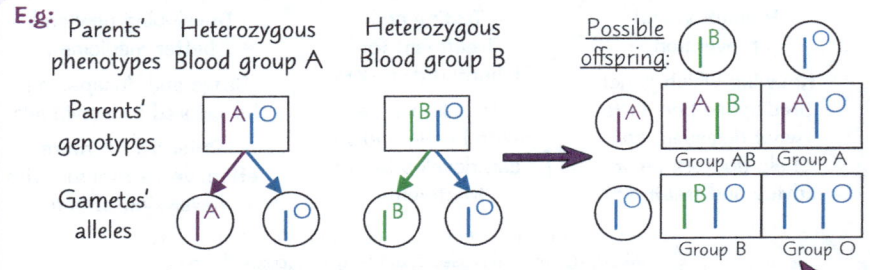

The child has an equal chance (1 in 4 or 25%) of having each blood group.

Variation & the Human Genome Project

Variation

VARIATION — differences in the characteristics of organisms.

Genetic variation

Differences in the genes individuals inherit cause genetic variation within a population — this is variation from *sexual reproduction*.

Mutations cause these differences in genes.

E.g. eye colour

There's lots of variation within species due to mutations.

	Most mutations	Some mutations	Very few mutations
Effect on phenotype	None	Slight	Significant

Environmental variation

Differences in the conditions in which organisms develop cause variation — they get *acquired characteristics*.

E.g. leaf colour

Genetic and environmental variation

For most characteristics, variation is caused by both genetics and the environment.

E.g. plant height

The Human Genome Project

The complete human genome has been worked out. Genes linked to diseases can be identified. This helps with...

Prediction and prevention
Knowing which genes predispose people to what diseases, can help doctors tailor advice and treatment.

Testing and treatment for inherited disorders
People can be tested early and we can develop better treatments.

Developing new and better medicines
Drugs and dosages can be tailored to individuals. Potential for more effective treatments with fewer side-effects.

Linking genes to diseases could lead to increased stress, gene-ism or discrimination by employers and insurers.

Topic 3 — Genetics

Topic 4 — Natural Selection and Genetic Modification

Natural Selection and Evolution

Evolution by Natural Selection

Darwin came up with the theory of evolution by natural selection.

EVOLUTION — the slow and continuous change of organisms from one generation to the next.

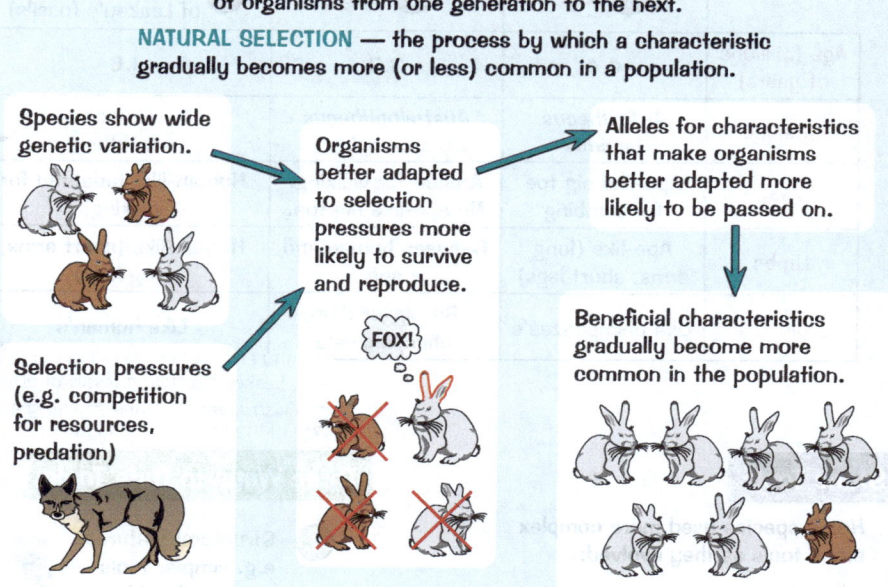

NATURAL SELECTION — the process by which a characteristic gradually becomes more (or less) common in a population.

- Species show wide genetic variation.
- Selection pressures (e.g. competition for resources, predation)
- Organisms better adapted to selection pressures more likely to survive and reproduce.
- Alleles for characteristics that make organisms better adapted more likely to be passed on.
- Beneficial characteristics gradually become more common in the population.

Antibiotic-Resistant Bacteria

Antibiotic resistance in bacteria supports Darwin's theory of evolution.

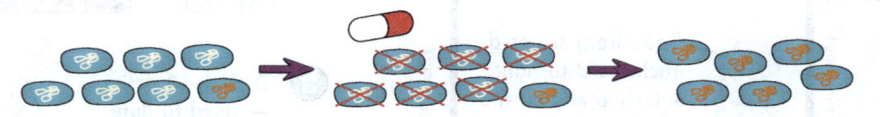

- Random mutations mean some bacteria develop allele for antibiotic resistance.
- Resistant bacteria survive the antibiotic and reproduce.
- Resistance allele more common in population.

> The emergence of other resistant organisms (e.g. rats resistant to poison) also supports Darwin's theory.

Evidence for Human Evolution

Hominid Fossils

Three fossils that provide evidence for human evolution:

'Ardi' and 'Lucy' were found in Ethiopia and Leakey's fossils were found in Kenya.

	1. Ardi	2. Lucy	3. Turkana Boy (one of Leakey's fossils)
Age (millions of years)	4.4	3.2	1.6
Species	*Ardipithecus ramidus*	*Australopithecus afarensis*	*Homo erectus*
Feet	Ape-like big toe for climbing	Arched for walking. No ape-like big toe.	Human-like (adapted for walking)
Limbs	Ape-like (long arms, short legs)	Between human and ape	Human-like (short arms, long legs)
Brain size	Like chimpanzee's	Bit bigger than chimpanzee's	Like human's

Leakey also found fossils of other *Australopithecus* and *Homo* species.

Stone Tools

Homo species used more complex stone tools as they evolved:

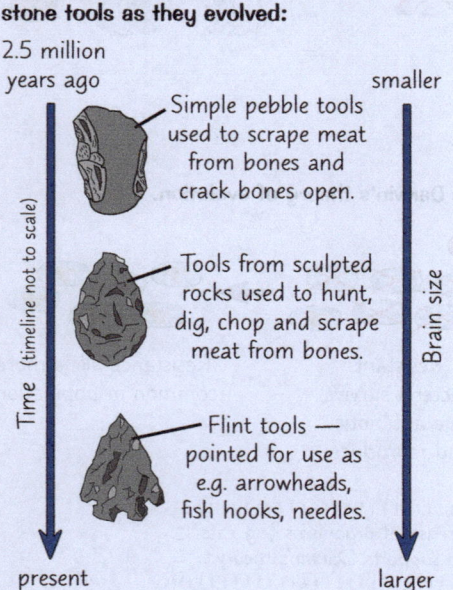

2.5 million years ago → present (Time, timeline not to scale)

- Simple pebble tools used to scrape meat from bones and crack bones open.
- Tools from sculpted rocks used to hunt, dig, chop and scrape meat from bones.
- Flint tools — pointed for use as e.g. arrowheads, fish hooks, needles.

Brain size: smaller → larger

Three Ways to Date Tools

1. **Structural features**, e.g. simpler tools are usually older.

2. **Rock layers** — deeper layer = older tool

3. **Carbon-14 dating** — used to date carbon-containing material found with tool.

I once dated a tool... It broke my heart.

Topic 4 — Natural Selection and Genetic Modification

Evidence and Theories of Evolution

Pentadactyl Limbs

PENTADACTYL LIMB — limb with five digits.

Similarities in structure of pentadactyl limbs of different species show they all evolved from a common ancestor.

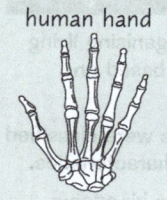

human hand — bat wing

Charles Darwin

Known for: the theory of evolution by natural selection.
Published: On the Origin of Species (1859)
Research: a world expedition studying plants and animals.

Observations:
- there is variation within species,
- individuals with characteristics most suited to environment are more likely to survive,
- characteristics can be passed on to offspring.

Alfred Russel Wallace

Known for: coming up with idea of natural selection, independently of Darwin.
Published: joint writings with Darwin on evolution.

Observations:

evidence for evolution by natural selection, e.g. warning colours are used by some species to deter predators from eating them.

Three Impacts on Modern Biology

The theory of evolution by natural selection has impacted:

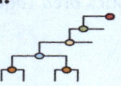

1. **Classification** — we now group organisms based on how closely related they are.

2. **Antibiotic use** — we now know how bacteria evolve to be antibiotic-resistant, so we know to finish a course of antibiotics and to constantly develop new ones.

3. **Conservation** — we now know the importance of maintaining genetic diversity within species so they can adapt to changing environments.

Topic 4 — Natural Selection and Genetic Modification

Classification and Selective Breeding

Traditional Classification System

CLASSIFICATION — organising living organisms into groups based on their features.

Traditionally, organisms were classified based on observable characteristics.

They were split into five kingdoms...

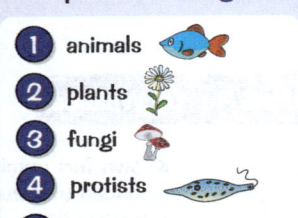

1. animals
2. plants
3. fungi
4. protists
5. prokaryotes

...then subdivided into smaller groups.

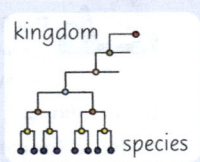

Modern Classification System

Now, organisms' genes can be analysed — the more similar the base sequence of a gene, the more closely related the organisms.

Organisms are now split into three domains before being subdivided into the smaller groups of the five kingdom system.

1	Bacteria	true bacteria
2	Archaea	a different type of prokaryotic cell first found in extreme places
3	Eukarya	including protists, fungi, plants and animals

Selective Breeding

SELECTIVE BREEDING — breeding plants or animals for particular characteristics (e.g. disease resistance in crops or a gentle temperament in dogs).

Individuals with desired characteristics bred together. → Repeated over generations. → Eventually all offspring have desired characteristics.

Benefits:
- **Agriculture**: crops and animals can be bred to produce bigger yields, e.g. more meat.
- **Medical research**: e.g. scientists can breed organisms with a characteristic they want to study.

Risks:
- **Less genetic variation** in population means it could be wiped out by an environmental change, e.g. a new disease.
- **Inbreeding** can cause health problems.

Topic 4 — Natural Selection and Genetic Modification

Genetic Engineering

Genetic Engineering Process

GENETIC ENGINEERING — transfer of a gene responsible for a desirable characteristic from one organism's genome into another organism.

It produces genetically modified organisms (GMOs).

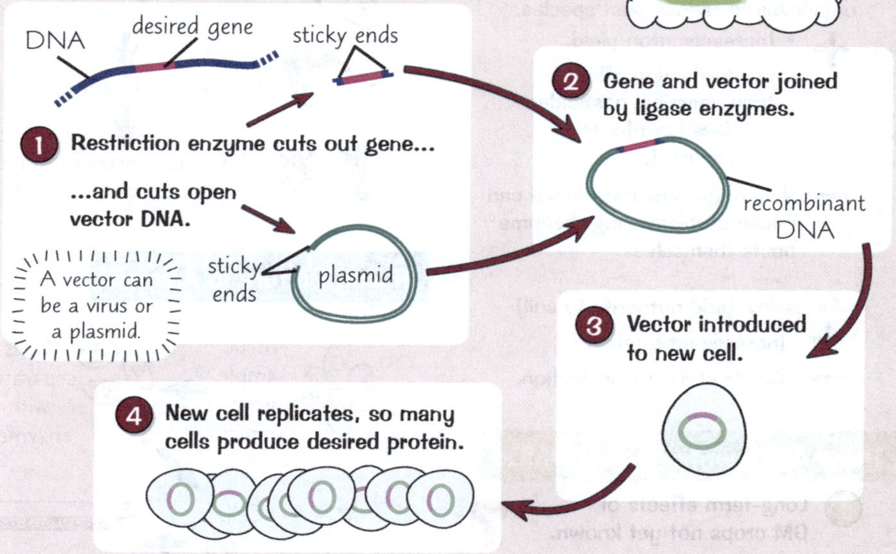

1. Restriction enzyme cuts out gene...
   ...and cuts open vector DNA.
   A vector can be a virus or a plasmid.

2. Gene and vector joined by ligase enzymes. → recombinant DNA

3. Vector introduced to new cell.

4. New cell replicates, so many cells produce desired protein.

Benefits and Risks of Genetic Engineering

Benefits:

Agriculture:
Can make crops resistant to drought, pests or herbicides.

Medicine:
Bacteria produce human insulin, which is used to treat diabetes.

Sheep and cows could produce human antibodies to treat illnesses, e.g. arthritis.

Risks:

Some GM animals have health problems.

GM crops could negatively affect food chains, or transplanted genes could get out into environment.

The antibodies are extracted from the animal, e.g. from its milk.

Topic 4 — Natural Selection and Genetic Modification

World Food Supply & Tissue Culture

Increasing Food Production

The world's population is rising, so we need ways to make sure there's enough food for everyone.

BIOLOGICAL CONTROL — using other organisms to reduce pest species.
- **+** Increases crop yield.
- **+** Longer-lasting effects than chemical pesticides and less harmful to environment.
- **−** New organisms introduced can cause problems, e.g. become pests themselves.

Fertilisers (add nutrients to soil)
- **+** Increase crop growth.
- **−** Can lead to eutrophication.

Three Arguments Against GMOs

1. Long-term effects of GM crops not yet known.
2. Countries may become dependent on companies that sell GM seeds.
3. People still might not be able to afford food — poverty should be tackled first.

Feeding the World — GMOs

Some crops are modified to provide more nutrients. GM drought- or pest-resistant crops can improve crop yields. E.g.

- *Bacillus thuringiensis* (Bt) has gene for toxin that kills insects.
- Bt gene inserted into crops.
- Crops now insect-resistant, so more food produced.

Tissue Culture in Animals

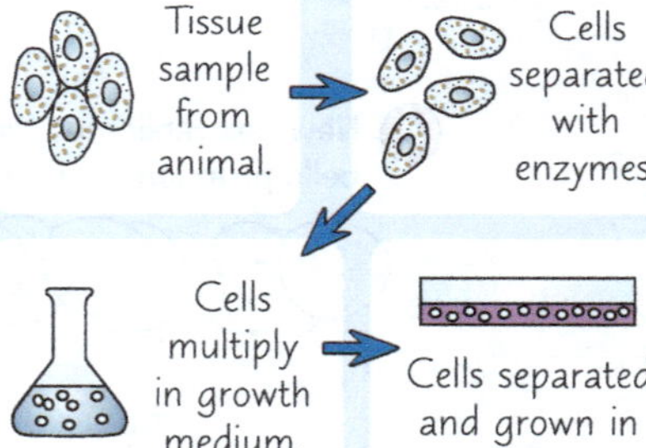

- Tissue sample from animal.
- Cells separated with enzymes.
- Cells separated and grown in culture vessel.
- Cells multiply in growth medium.

+ **Medical research** can be done on isolated tissues, without complications from other life processes.

Tissue Culture in Plants

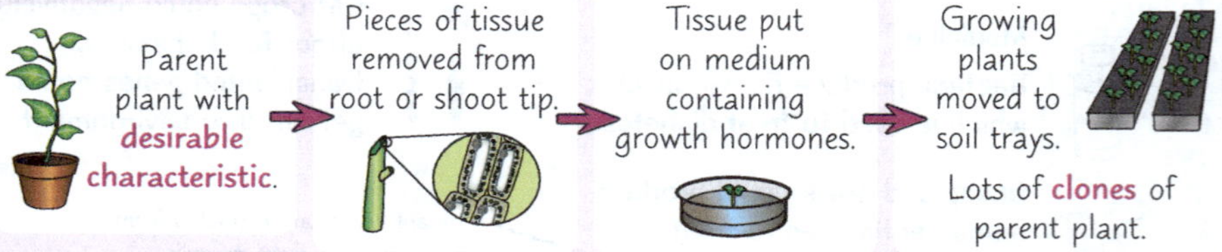

- Parent plant with **desirable characteristic**.
- Pieces of tissue removed from root or shoot tip.
- Tissue put on medium containing growth hormones.
- Growing plants moved to soil trays. Lots of **clones** of parent plant.

+ Plants with same beneficial features made quickly, all year, in little space.

Topic 4 — Natural Selection and Genetic Modification

Topic 5 — Health, Disease & the Development of Medicines

Health and Disease

Health

HEALTH — a state of complete physical, mental and social well-being, and not merely the absence of disease or infirmity.

Diseases can cause ill health.

Having a disease can weaken your body, making you more susceptible to other diseases.

Two Types of Disease

1. **COMMUNICABLE DISEASE** — a disease that can spread from person to person or between animals and people.

2. **NON-COMMUNICABLE DISEASE** — a disease that cannot spread between people or between animals and people.

Viruses

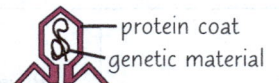

- protein coat
- genetic material
- Viruses are not cells.
- They infect living cells to reproduce.

Viral life cycle:

1. virus attaches to host cell and injects genetic material
2. viral DNA replicates using proteins and enzymes in host cell
3. new viruses are assembled
4. host cell splits, releasing viruses

Lytic Pathway

host cell
host cell DNA

Lysogenic Pathway

1. viral DNA is incorporated in host cell genome
2. viral DNA replicates when host cell divides but no new viruses made — virus is inactive
3. trigger (e.g. a chemical) causes viral genetic material to leave the genome and enter lytic pathway

Communicable Diseases

Infectious Diseases

PATHOGENS — organisms that cause communicable diseases.

Disease	Pathogen	How it's spread	Signs / symptoms	Ways to reduce spread
Chalara ash dieback	Fungus	• Wind • Transfer of diseased trees	• Leaf loss • Bark lesions (wounds)	• Remove infected ash trees • Restrict imports
Malaria	Protist	Mosquito vectors	• Damage to red blood cells • Damage to liver	• Mosquito nets • Insect repellent
Cholera	Bacterium	Contaminated water sources	Diarrhoea	Have clean water supplies
Tuberculosis	Bacterium	Airborne droplets (coughs and sneezes)	• Coughing • Lung damage	Infected people should: • Avoid crowds • Sleep alone • Ventilate homes
Stomach ulcers	Bacterium (*Helicobacter pylori*)	Oral transmission	• Stomach pain • Nausea • Vomiting	• Have clean water supplies • Hygienic living conditions
Ebola	Virus	Exchanging bodily fluids (e.g. blood)	Haemorrhagic fever ↑ fever with bleeding	• Isolate infected individuals • Sterilise areas

Topic 5 — Health, Disease & the Development of Medicines

STIs and Defences Against Disease

Sexually Transmitted Infections (STIs)

SEXUALLY TRANSMITTED INFECTION — infection spread through sexual contact.

STI	Pathogen	How it's spread	Symptoms / effects	Ways to reduce spread
Chlamydia	Bacterium	Sexual contact, including genital contact	• Often none • Can cause infertility	• Wear a condom • Screen individuals • Avoid sexual contact
HIV	Virus	Exchanging bodily fluids (e.g. blood, semen)	• Kills white blood cells • Reduces immune response • Leads to AIDS • Vulnerability to other infections	• Wear a condom • Avoid sharing needles • Take medication • Screen individuals

Human Defences Against Disease

PHYSICAL BARRIERS

Skin acts as a barrier to pathogens.

Hairs and **mucus** in the nose trap particles containing pathogens.

Mucus in trachea and bronchi traps pathogens, and **cilia** waft mucus up to throat so it can be swallowed.

CHEMICAL BARRIERS

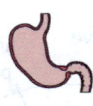

Hydrochloric acid in the stomach kills pathogens.

Lysozymes in tears kill bacteria.

Topic 5 — Health, Disease & the Development of Medicines

The Immune System

Specific Immune Response

SPECIFIC IMMUNE RESPONSE — the immune response to a specific pathogen.

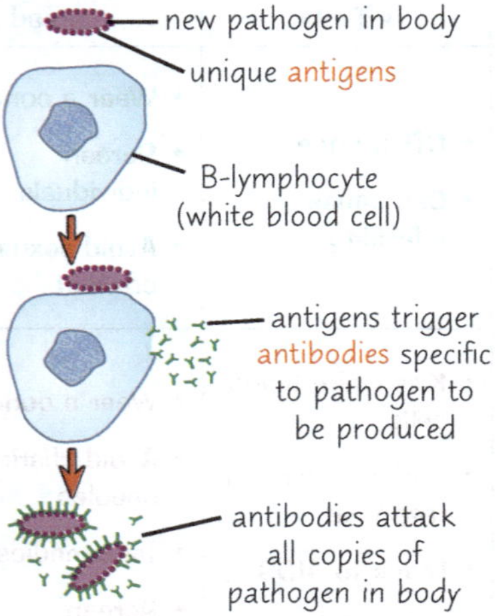

- new pathogen in body
- unique antigens
- B-lymphocyte (white blood cell)
- antigens trigger antibodies specific to pathogen to be produced
- antibodies attack all copies of pathogen in body

Memory lymphocytes also produced — these stay in body for long time and 'remember' antigen.

Secondary Immune Response

Key: ● exposure to antigen

First immune response — slow.

Secondary immune response — **faster** and **stronger**. Memory lymphocytes trigger fast production of antibodies.

Axes: Antibodies in blood vs Time / days (10, 20, 30, long interval)

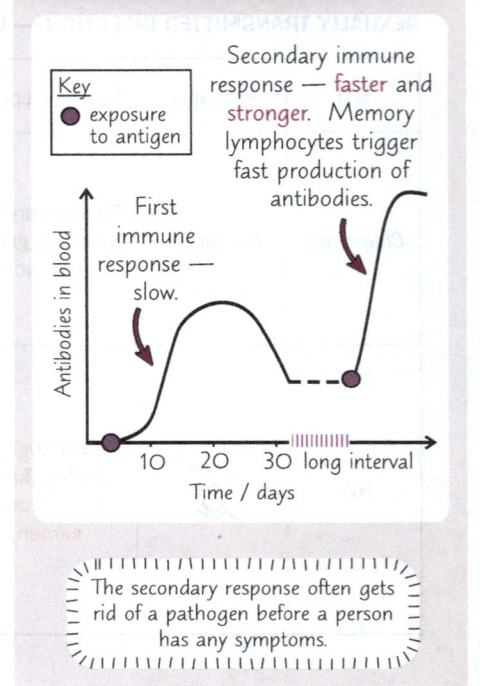

The secondary response often gets rid of a pathogen before a person has any symptoms.

Immunisation

IMMUNISATION — a process that makes an individual resistant to becoming ill from a specific communicable disease.

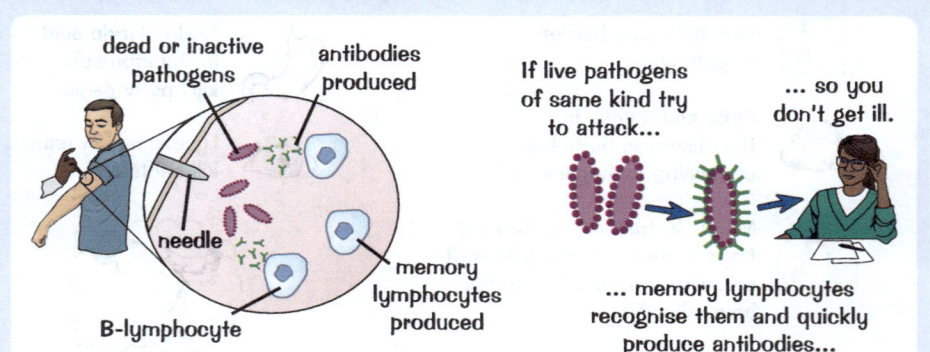

- dead or inactive pathogens
- needle
- B-lymphocyte
- antibodies produced
- memory lymphocytes produced

If live pathogens of same kind try to attack...

... so you don't get ill.

... memory lymphocytes recognise them and quickly produce antibodies...

Topic 5 — Health, Disease & the Development of Medicines

Immunisation and Plant Diseases

Advantages and Disadvantages of Immunisation

Advantages
- Prevents individuals getting ill.
- Can create herd immunity (where high percentage of population is immunised so spread of disease is limited, meaning large outbreak of disease unlikely).
- Has almost wiped out some diseases.

Disadvantages
- It doesn't always work.
- Bad reactions to vaccine possible.

Jo admitted her reaction could have been better...

Plant Defences Against Pests and Pathogens

Physical	Chemical
Waxy cuticle on leaves — barrier to pests and pathogens.	Antiseptic chemicals kill bacterial and fungal pathogens.
Cellulose cell walls — barrier to pathogens around cells.	Some plants produce chemicals to deter pests from feeding on them.

Some plant chemicals are used as drugs to treat human diseases or relieve symptoms, e.g. quinine for malaria.

Four Ways to Detect or Identify Plant Disease

1. **Observation** — look at plant's symptoms and identify the disease.

2. **Experimentation** — alter plant's environmental conditions and observe any changes (to see if environment is causing plant's symptoms, rather than a pathogen).

3. **Analysing distribution** — identify the disease by looking at distribution of affected plants (e.g. random distribution suggests airborne pathogen).

4. **Diagnostic testing** — test sample of plant tissue in lab for presence of particular pathogen. E.g.:
   - Use monoclonal antibodies to detect antigens from the pathogen.
   - Test for the pathogen's DNA.

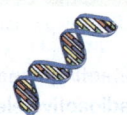

Topic 5 — Health, Disease & the Development of Medicines

Monoclonal Antibodies

Monoclonal Antibodies

Monoclonal antibodies are produced from lots of clones of a single white blood cell (a B-lymphocyte).

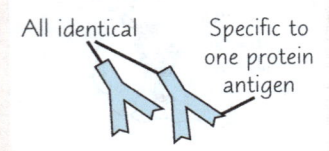

Monoclonal antibodies
- All identical
- Specific to one protein antigen

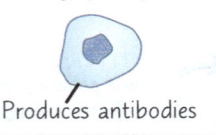

B-lymphocyte
- Produces antibodies

Producing Monoclonal Antibodies

Mouse injected with chosen antigen

Tumour cells in lab — don't make antibodies but divide lots

B-lymphocytes from mouse — make antibodies but don't divide easily

B-lymphocyte fused with tumour cell

antibodies specific to injected antigen

This makes a **hybridoma**.

It divides quickly to produce lots of clones that produce the monoclonal antibodies. → monoclonal antibodies

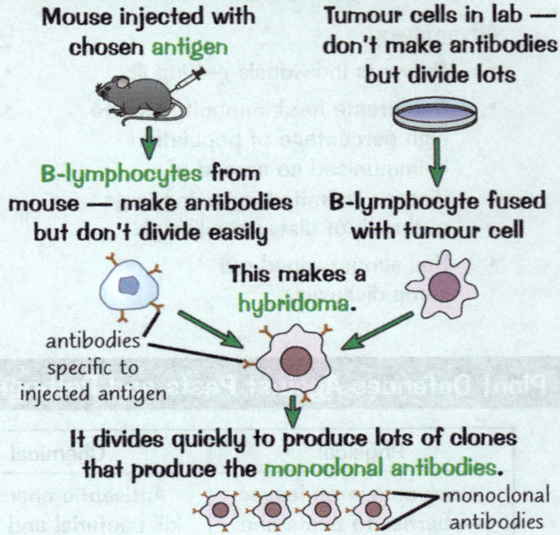

Three Uses of Monoclonal Antibodies

1. Pregnancy tests

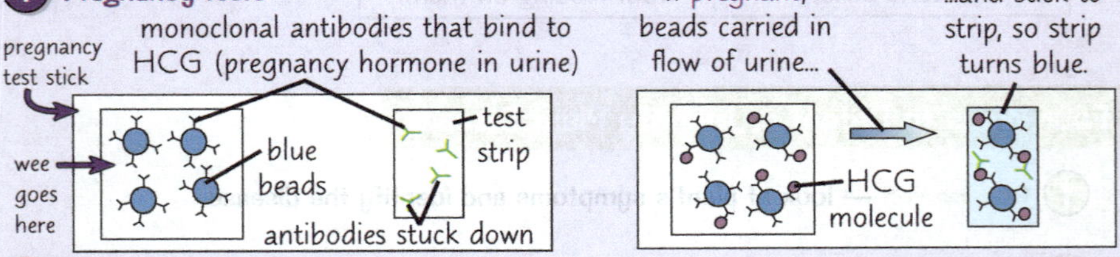

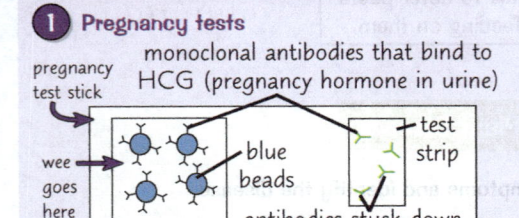

monoclonal antibodies that bind to HCG (pregnancy hormone in urine)

- pregnancy test stick
- wee goes here
- blue beads
- test strip
- antibodies stuck down

If pregnant, beads carried in flow of urine... ...and stick to strip, so strip turns blue.

- HCG molecule

2. Treating cancer

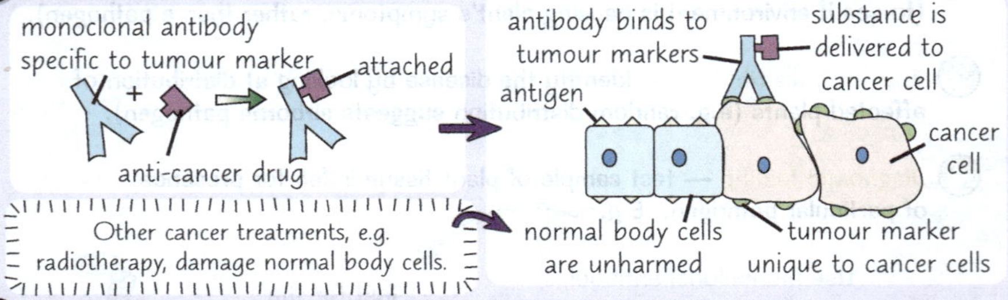

monoclonal antibody specific to tumour marker + anti-cancer drug → attached

antibody binds to tumour markers antigen

substance is delivered to cancer cell

- cancer cell
- normal body cells are unharmed
- tumour marker unique to cancer cells

Other cancer treatments, e.g. radiotherapy, damage normal body cells.

3. Detecting cancer cells and blood clots

Radioactive element attached to monoclonal antibodies that bind to tumour markers or proteins in clot. Location of radioactivity then found with a special camera.

Topic 5 — Health, Disease & the Development of Medicines

Medicines and Lifestyle Factors

Antibiotics

- Antibiotics only kill bacteria.
- They inhibit processes in bacterial cells, but not in the host organism.

Developing New Medicines

Discovery — Scientists use knowledge of how disease works to identify molecules that could be used to treat it. New drug is then developed through testing.

Preclinical Testing
- Tests on human cells and tissues → Tests on live animals

Clinical Testing
- Tests on healthy volunteers
- The dosage is gradually increased from a very low initial dose
- Tests on ill patients
- Finding optimum dose

Clinical trials are often double-blind
- Given drug
- Given placebo

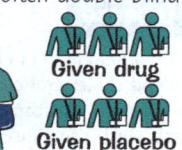

PLACEBOS — substances that are like the drug being tested but don't do anything.

New drug approved by medical agency when tests show it's safe and effective.

Four Risk Factors for Non-Communicable Diseases

RISK FACTORS — things that are linked to an increase in the likelihood that a person will develop a certain disease during their lifetime.

1. A lack of exercise is linked to cardiovascular disease and obesity.

2. A poor diet with too few or too many nutrients can lead to malnutrition or related disorders, e.g. obesity, scurvy (lack of vitamin C).

3. Drinking too much alcohol can cause liver disease and cardiovascular disease.

4. Smoking can cause cardiovascular disease, lung disease and lung cancer. It is also linked to other types of cancer.

Many non-communicable diseases are caused by several risk factors interacting.

Topic 5 — Health, Disease & the Development of Medicines

Non-Communicable Diseases

Effects of Non-Communicable Diseases

1. **Local** — high levels of disease puts pressure on local hospitals.

2. **National** — expensive for NHS to treat everyone and reduces number of people who can work (affects economy).

3. **Global** — costs associated with high levels of disease can hold back a country's development.

Two Measures of Obesity

1. $\text{BMI} = \dfrac{\text{mass (kg)}}{(\text{height (m)})^2}$

   Result is used to classify body, e.g. < 18.5 = underweight, > 30 = obese.

2. $\text{Waist-to-hip ratio} = \dfrac{\text{waist circumference (cm)}}{\text{hip circumference (cm)}}$

   A ratio above 1.0 (men) and 0.85 (women) indicates abdominal obesity, which increases the risk of other health problems.

Three Ways of Treating Cardiovascular Disease

CARDIOVASCULAR DISEASE (CVD) — any disease associated with the heart and blood vessels.

Too much blood cholesterol can cause fatty deposits to build up in arteries. This can lead to a blood clot and blocked vessel, which can cause a heart attack or stroke.

Treatment	Advantages	Disadvantages
1. **Lifestyle changes** (e.g. exercise)	Reduces risk of heart attack and stroke.	None.
2. **Life-long medication** — Statins	Reduce cholesterol, slowing down formation of fatty deposits.	Side effects, including possible liver damage.
Anticoagulants	Make blood clots less likely.	Can cause excessive bleeding.
Antihypertensives	Reduce blood pressure, limiting damage to blood vessels.	Side effects, e.g. headaches, fainting.
3. **Surgical procedures** — Stent (tube put in artery)	Keeps arteries open so blood flow isn't blocked.	• Scar tissue may form. • Have to take drugs to stop blood clotting.
Coronary bypass surgery (healthy blood vessel put in heart)	Reduces risk of heart attack.	Heart surgery is a major procedure — risk of bleeding, clots, infection.
Donor heart	Can treat heart failure.	• Risks from surgery. • Drugs have to be taken to stop body rejecting it.

Topic 5 — Health, Disease & the Development of Medicines

Photosynthesis

The Photosynthesis Reaction

PHOTOSYNTHESIS — an endothermic reaction that happens in plants and algae, in which energy is transferred to chloroplasts from the environment by light.

$$\text{carbon dioxide} + \text{water} \xrightarrow{\text{light}} \text{glucose} + \text{oxygen}$$

Photosynthetic organisms make biomass from glucose. The energy in the biomass is passed on through food chains, so photosynthetic organisms are the **main producers** of food for nearly all life on Earth.

Three Limiting Factors of Photosynthesis

LIMITING FACTOR (of photosynthesis) — thing that stops photosynthesis happening any faster.

1. Temperature

temperature is limiting factor — enzymes work slowly at low temperatures

(Rate vs Temperature (°C), peak at 45)

high temperatures denature enzymes involved in photosynthesis

2. CO_2 concentration

CO_2 concentration is limiting factor

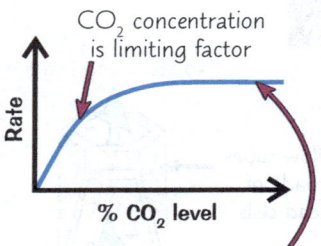

(Rate vs % CO_2 level)

temperature or light intensity are limiting factors

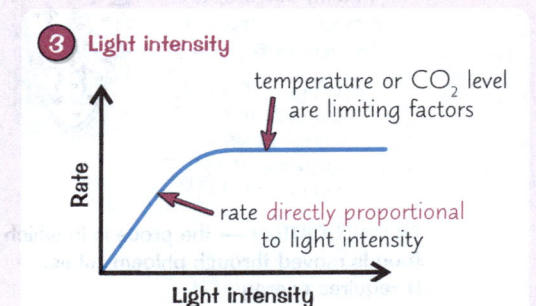

3. Light intensity

temperature or CO_2 level are limiting factors

(Rate vs Light intensity)

rate *directly proportional* to light intensity

Light intensity and the distance from a light source are **inversely proportional** to each other.

The **inverse square law** links light intensity with distance from a light source:

$$\text{Light intensity} \propto \frac{1}{\text{distance}\,(d)^2}$$

E.g. doubling the distance means light intensity is four times smaller.

Plant Cells

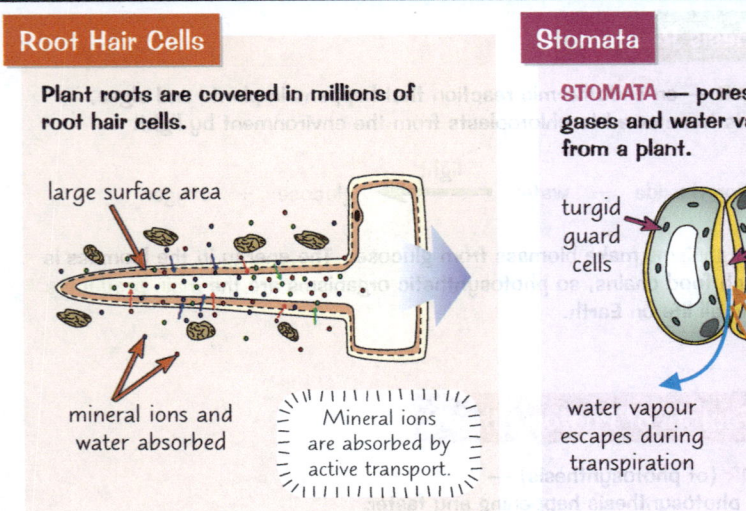

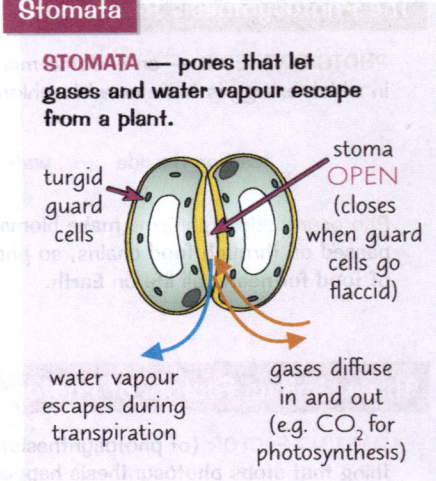

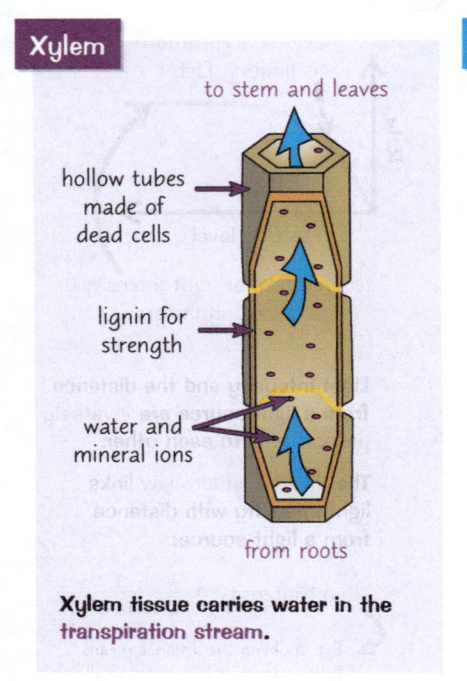

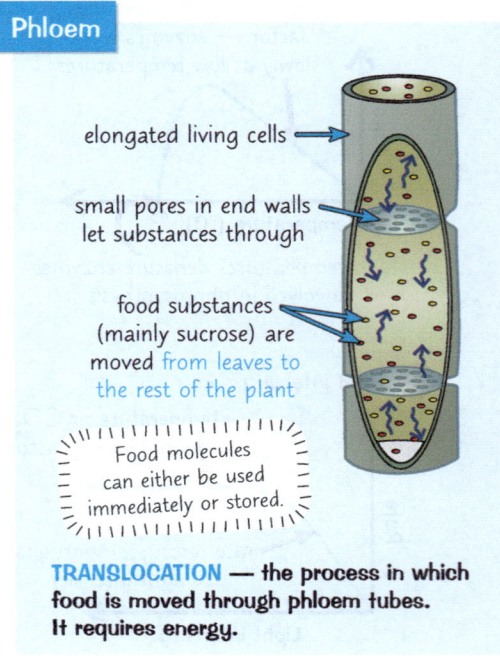

Root Hair Cells

Plant roots are covered in millions of root hair cells.

- large surface area
- mineral ions and water absorbed

Mineral ions are absorbed by active transport.

Stomata

STOMATA — pores that let gases and water vapour escape from a plant.

- turgid guard cells
- stoma OPEN (closes when guard cells go flaccid)
- water vapour escapes during transpiration
- gases diffuse in and out (e.g. CO_2 for photosynthesis)

Xylem

- to stem and leaves
- hollow tubes made of dead cells
- lignin for strength
- water and mineral ions
- from roots

Xylem tissue carries water in the transpiration stream.

Phloem

- elongated living cells
- small pores in end walls let substances through
- food substances (mainly sucrose) are moved from leaves to the rest of the plant

Food molecules can either be used immediately or stored.

TRANSLOCATION — the process in which food is moved through phloem tubes. It requires energy.

Topic 6 — Plant Structures and Their Functions

Transpiration

Transpiration Basics

TRANSPIRATION — the loss of water from a plant.

Water evaporates and diffuses out of the plant...

...which causes more water to be drawn into the plant from the roots.

Mineral ions are carried in the transpiration stream.

It transpired that Jay did indeed have a favourite plant.

Transpiration Rate

These three things increase transpiration rate:

1. **Warm temperatures** 

   Water molecules have more energy.

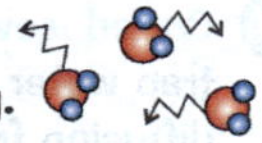

2. **High light intensity** 

   Stomata open when it's light.

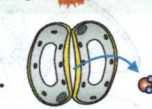

3. **Good air flow** 

   Fewer water molecules surround the leaves (so there's a higher water concentration inside the leaf than outside it).

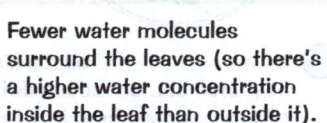

Transpiration Rate Calculations

Potometer used to estimate transpiration rate:

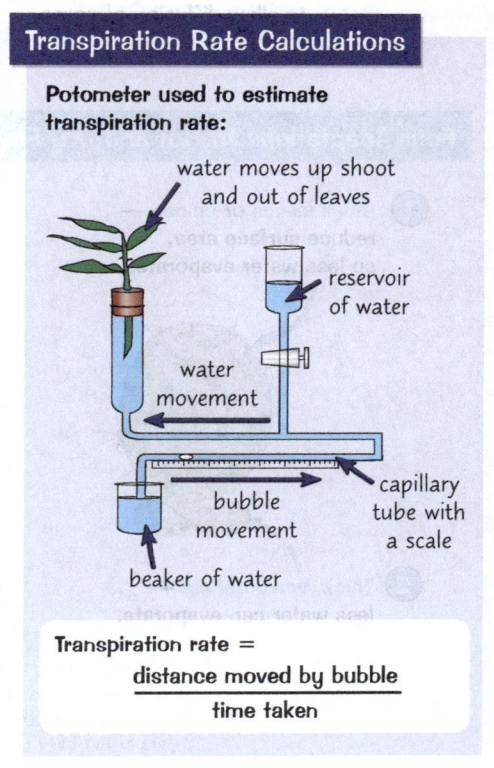

- water moves up shoot and out of leaves
- reservoir of water
- water movement
- bubble movement
- capillary tube with a scale
- beaker of water

$$\text{Transpiration rate} = \frac{\text{distance moved by bubble}}{\text{time taken}}$$

Topic 6 — Plant Structures and Their Functions

Adaptations of Leaves and Plants

Eight Adaptations of Leaves for Photosynthesis and Gas Exchange

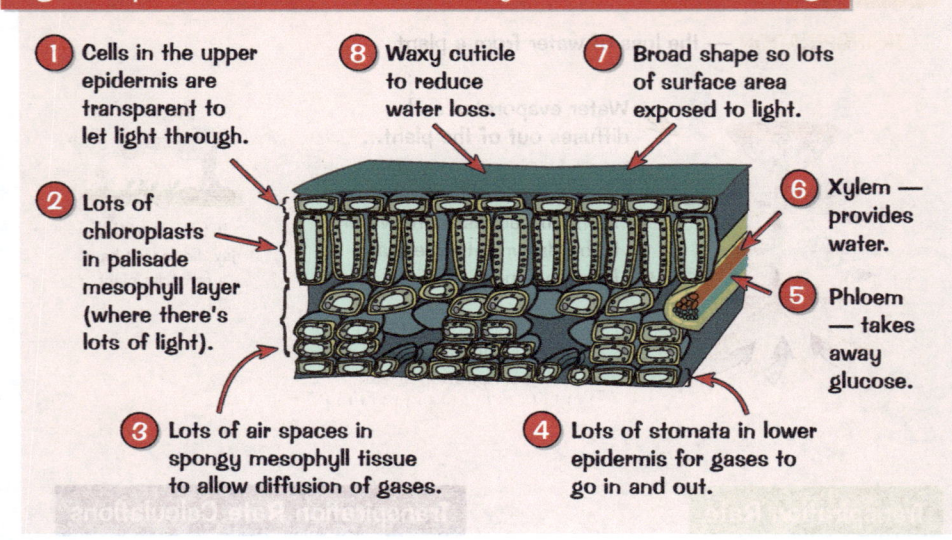

1. Cells in the upper epidermis are transparent to let light through.
2. Lots of chloroplasts in palisade mesophyll layer (where there's lots of light).
3. Lots of air spaces in spongy mesophyll tissue to allow diffusion of gases.
4. Lots of stomata in lower epidermis for gases to go in and out.
5. Phloem — takes away glucose.
6. Xylem — provides water.
7. Broad shape so lots of surface area exposed to light.
8. Waxy cuticle to reduce water loss.

Four Adaptations to Hot and Dry Environments

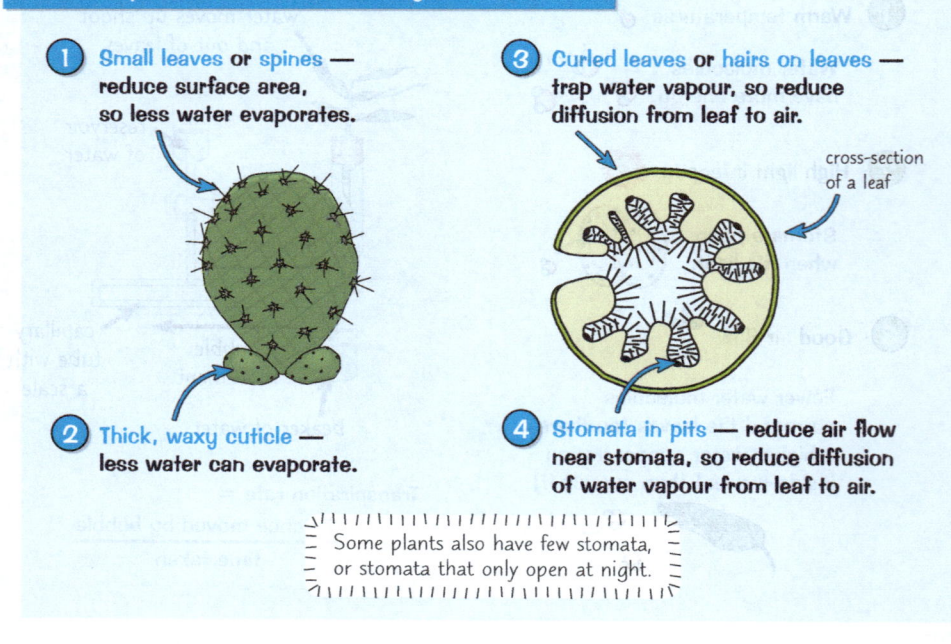

1. **Small leaves** or **spines** — reduce surface area, so less water evaporates.
2. **Thick, waxy cuticle** — less water can evaporate.
3. **Curled leaves** or **hairs on leaves** — trap water vapour, so reduce diffusion from leaf to air.
4. **Stomata in pits** — reduce air flow near stomata, so reduce diffusion of water vapour from leaf to air.

cross-section of a leaf

Some plants also have few stomata, or stomata that only open at night.

Topic 6 — Plant Structures and Their Functions

Plant Hormones

Phototropism

AUXIN — a plant hormone that controls growth near the tips of shoots and roots.

Positive phototropism:

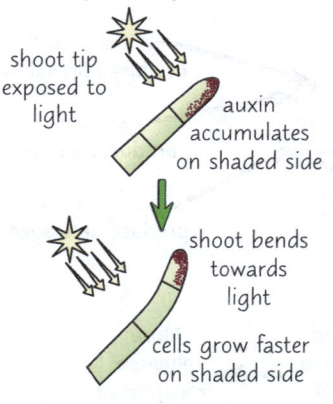

shoot tip exposed to light

auxin accumulates on shaded side

shoot bends towards light

cells grow faster on shaded side

Roots are negatively phototropic — they grow away from light.

Gravitropism

Negative gravitropism:

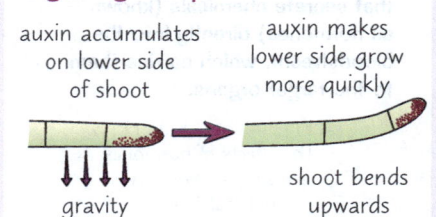

auxin accumulates on lower side of shoot

gravity

auxin makes lower side grow more quickly

shoot bends upwards

Positive gravitropism:

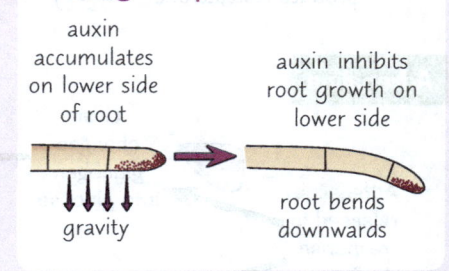

auxin accumulates on lower side of root

gravity

auxin inhibits root growth on lower side

root bends downwards

Commercial Uses of Plant Hormones

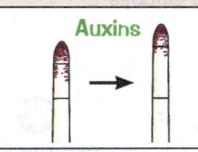

Auxins
- Developed to selectively kill weeds whilst leaving crops untouched
- Added to rooting powders to promote root growth in plant cuttings

Ethene
- Speeds up ripening of fruits in transport to shops

Aaaaand... AUXIN!

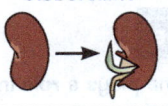

Gibberellins
- Stimulates seeds to germinate at any time of year
- Induces flowering without the need for specific conditions
- Reduces number of fruits produced, so each fruit can grow larger
- Can make unpollinated flowers produce seedless fruits

Topic 6 — Plant Structures and Their Functions

Hormones

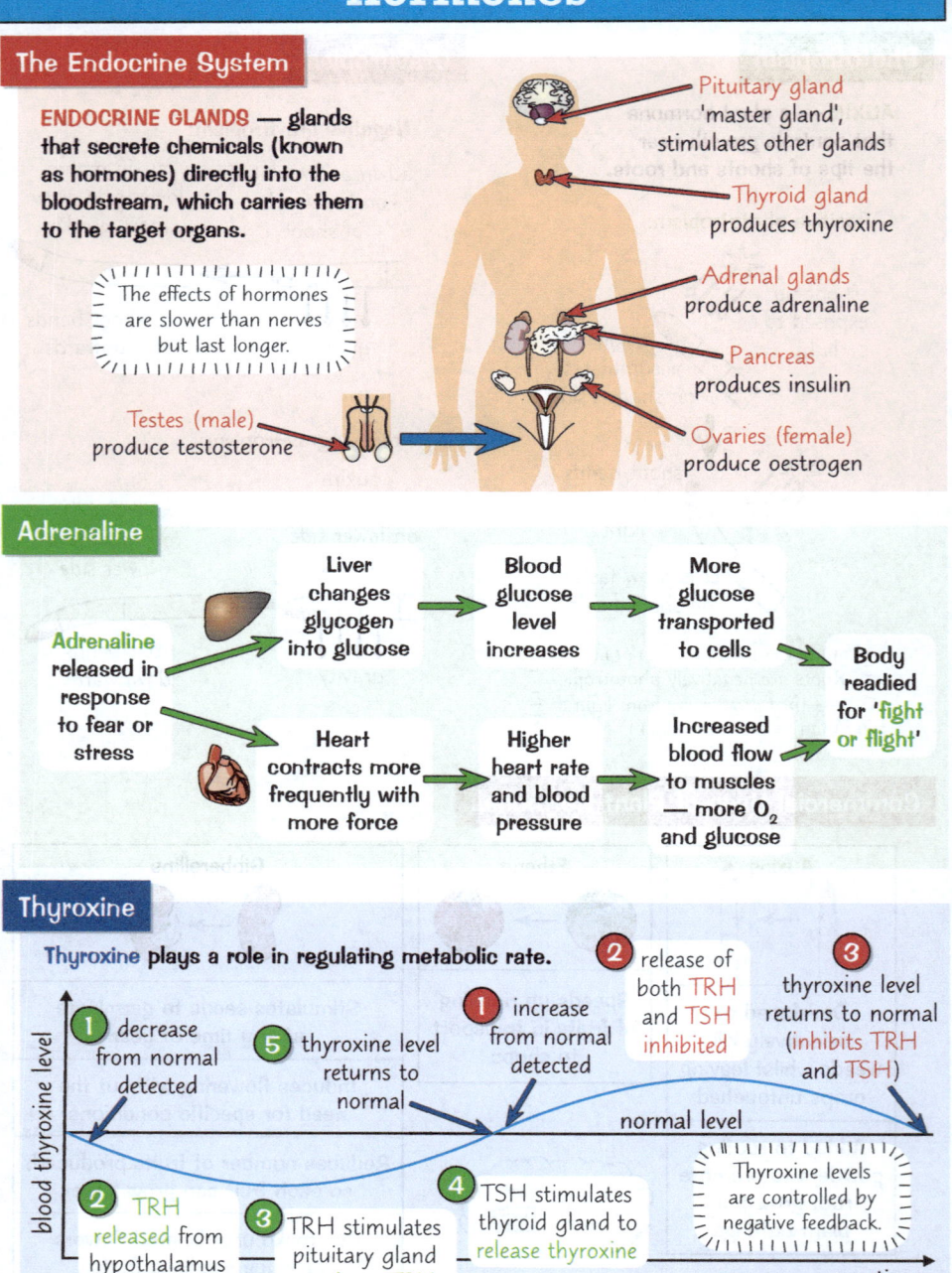

The Endocrine System

ENDOCRINE GLANDS — glands that secrete chemicals (known as hormones) directly into the bloodstream, which carries them to the target organs.

The effects of hormones are slower than nerves but last longer.

- **Pituitary gland** — 'master gland', stimulates other glands
- **Thyroid gland** — produces thyroxine
- **Adrenal glands** — produce adrenaline
- **Pancreas** — produces insulin
- **Testes (male)** — produce testosterone
- **Ovaries (female)** — produce oestrogen

Adrenaline

Adrenaline released in response to fear or stress →

- Liver changes glycogen into glucose → Blood glucose level increases → More glucose transported to cells → Body readied for 'fight or flight'
- Heart contracts more frequently with more force → Higher heart rate and blood pressure → Increased blood flow to muscles — more O_2 and glucose → Body readied for 'fight or flight'

Thyroxine

Thyroxine plays a role in regulating metabolic rate.

1. increase from normal detected
2. release of both TRH and TSH inhibited
3. thyroxine level returns to normal (inhibits TRH and TSH)
1. decrease from normal detected
2. TRH released from hypothalamus
3. TRH stimulates pituitary gland to release TSH
4. TSH stimulates thyroid gland to release thyroxine
5. thyroxine level returns to normal

Thyroxine levels are controlled by negative feedback.

(axes: blood thyroxine level vs time; normal level)

The Menstrual Cycle

Stages of the Menstrual Cycle

Day 1 — Day 4 — follicle matures — Day 14 — ovulation — corpus luteum — Day 28

FSH, LH, Oestrogen, Progesterone

Stage 1 — Uterus lining breaks down. Menstruation starts.

FSH (follicle-stimulating hormone) causes an egg to mature in an ovary.

Stage 2 — Uterus lining is repaired. Builds up into thick spongy layer full of blood vessels ready to receive a fertilised egg.

Oestrogen causes uterus lining to grow.

Stage 3 — Egg develops and is released from ovary (ovulation).

LH (luteinising hormone) stimulates ovulation.

Stage 4 — Lining is maintained. If no fertilised egg lands on wall, lining breaks down and cycle starts again.

Progesterone maintains uterus lining.

Next cycle

Hormone Feedback in the Menstrual Cycle

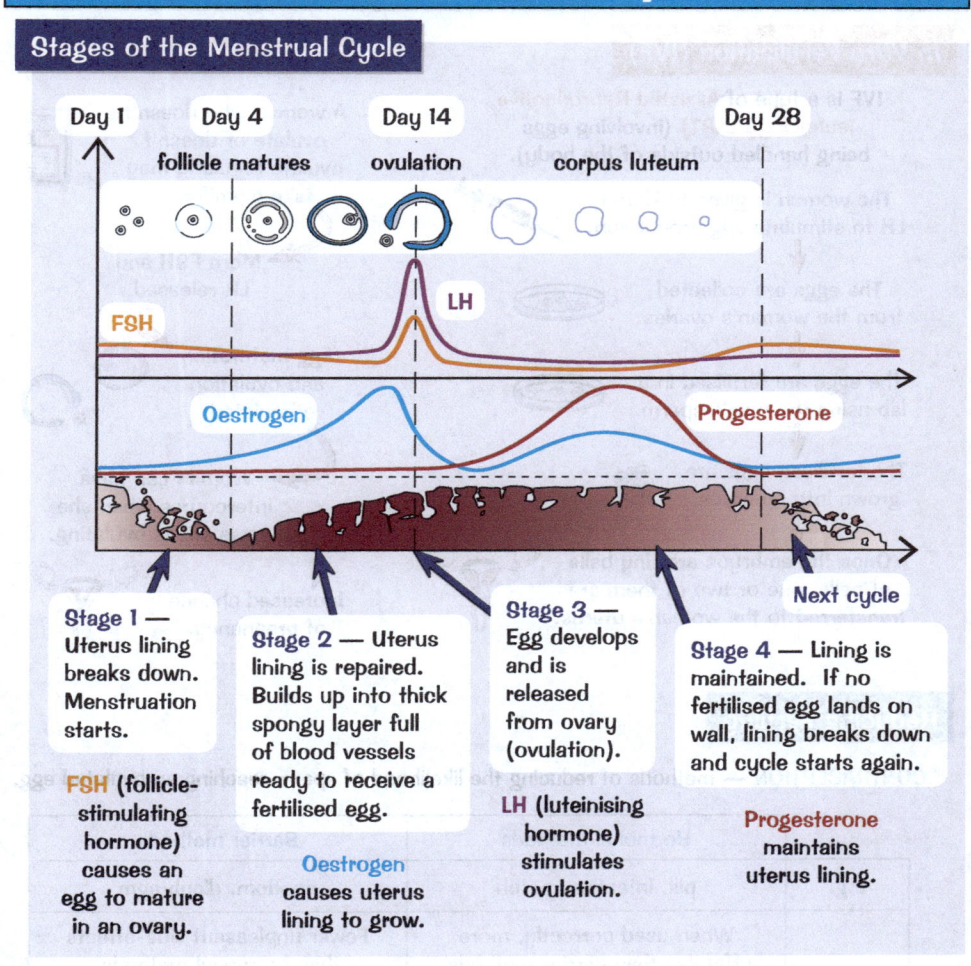

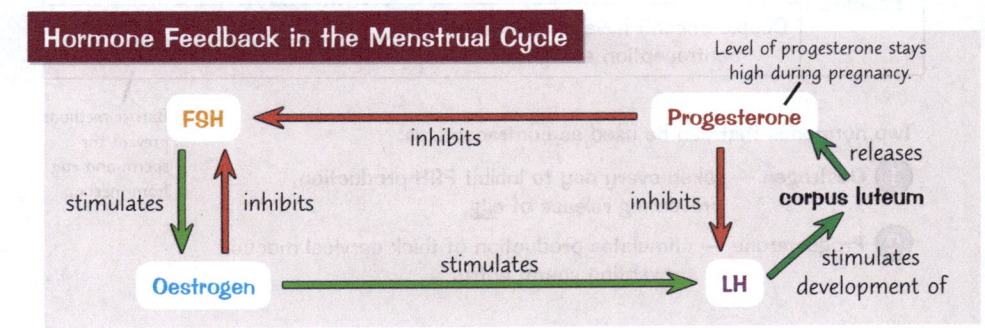

Level of progesterone stays high during pregnancy.

- FSH stimulates Oestrogen
- Oestrogen inhibits FSH
- Oestrogen stimulates LH
- LH stimulates development of corpus luteum
- corpus luteum releases Progesterone
- Progesterone inhibits FSH
- Progesterone inhibits LH

Topic 7 — Animal Coordination, Control & Homeostasis

Controlling Fertility

In Vitro Fertilisation (IVF)

IVF is a type of Assisted Reproductive Technology (ART) (involving eggs being handled outside of the body).

- The woman is given FSH and LH to stimulate egg production. 
- The eggs are collected from the woman's ovaries. 
- The eggs are fertilised in a lab using the man's sperm. 
- The fertilised eggs are grown into embryos.
- Once the embryos are tiny balls of cells, one or two of them are transferred to the woman's uterus.

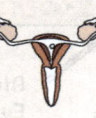

Clomifene Therapy

- A woman who doesn't ovulate or doesn't ovulate regularly may take clomifene. 
- More FSH and LH released.
- Egg maturation and ovulation stimulated. 
- Woman can have intercourse when she knows she is ovulating.
- Increased chance of pregnancy.

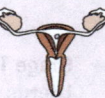

Reducing Fertility

CONTRACEPTION — methods of reducing the likelihood of sperm reaching an ovulated egg.

	Hormonal methods	Barrier methods
E.g.	pill, injection, patch	condom, diaphragm
Benefits	When used correctly, more effective than barrier methods.	Fewer unpleasant side-effects than hormonal methods.
	Couple doesn't have to think about contraception every time.	Condoms can protect against STIs.

Barrier methods prevent the sperm and egg from meeting.

Two hormones that can be used as contraceptives:

1. Oestrogen — taken every day to inhibit FSH production, preventing release of egg.
2. Progesterone — stimulates production of thick cervical mucus, preventing sperm entry.

Topic 7 — Animal Coordination, Control & Homeostasis

Homeostasis — Blood Glucose

Homeostasis

HOMEOSTASIS — the regulation of the conditions inside your body and cells. It maintains a stable internal environment in response to changes in internal and external conditions.

Stable internal environment in here.

It's important to maintain constant conditions for cells to function properly.

Controlling Blood Glucose

Five steps the body takes to reduce blood glucose:

1. Blood with too much glucose
2. Pancreas detects high blood glucose and secretes **insulin**
3. Insulin causes glucose to move into cells
4. Insulin makes the liver turn glucose into **glycogen**, which is stored in the liver and muscles
5. Blood glucose reduced

Five steps the body takes to increase blood glucose:

1. Blood with too little glucose
2. **Glucagon** secreted by the pancreas
3. Too little glucose but glucagon as well
4. Glucagon makes the liver turn glycogen into **glucose**, which is released from the liver
5. Blood glucose increased

Insulin and glucagon work in a **negative feedback cycle**.

Diabetes

	Type 1	Type 2
Cause	Pancreas produces little or no insulin	Cells no longer respond to insulin properly
Effect	Blood glucose can rise to dangerously high levels	
Treatment	Insulin therapy, e.g. injections	Healthy diet and regular exercise

There is a correlation between obesity and type 2 diabetes.
Two ways of measuring obesity:

1. $$BMI = \frac{mass\ (kg)}{(height\ (m))^2}$$ — BMI over 30 = obese

2. $$Waist\text{-}to\text{-}hip\ ratio = \frac{waist\ circumference\ (cm)}{hip\ circumference\ (cm)}$$

A ratio above 1.0 (men) and 0.85 (women) = increased risk of type 2 diabetes

Topic 7 — Animal Coordination, Control & Homeostasis

Thermoregulation & Osmoregulation

Controlling Body Temperature

Thermoregulation keeps the body at the optimum temperature for enzyme activity. Two locations of temperature receptors in the body:

1. In the thermoregulatory centre in the hypothalamus (in brain).
2. In the skin — in the epidermis (outer layer) and dermis (deeper layer).

Temperature receptors detect core body temperature is too **high** or too **low**. → body warms up / body cools down → Thermoregulatory centre receives information — triggers effectors. → Effectors produce response and counteract change.

Effectors in Thermoregulation

When you're **hot**, effectors help to transfer energy from the skin to the environment:
- hair erector muscle relaxes, so hair lies flat
- sweat gland releases sweat through pores in epidermis
- blood vessels dilate (**vasodilation**) and more blood flows close to surface

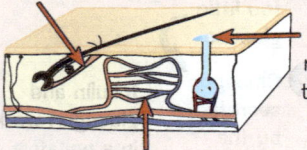

When you're **cold**, effectors reduce the energy transferred to the environment:
- erect hairs trap insulating layer of air
- epidermis
- dermis
- no sweat
- blood vessels constrict (**vasoconstriction**) and less blood flows close to surface
- **shivering** (muscles contracting) increases respiration rate

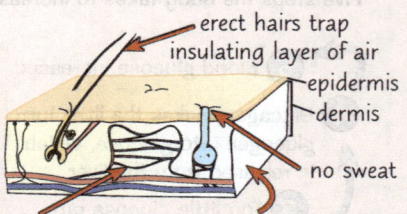

Regulating Water Content

Osmoregulation keeps the body's water content at the right level for cells to function.

Too high — water moves into cells and they burst.

Too low — water moves out of cells and they shrink.

The Urinary System

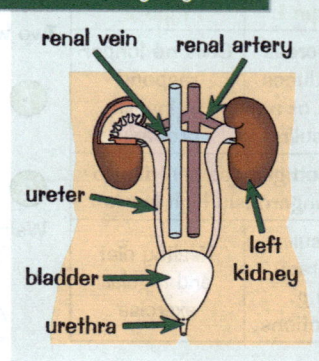

- renal vein
- renal artery
- ureter
- bladder
- left kidney
- urethra

Three roles of kidneys:
1. Removal of urea from blood.
2. Adjustment of ion levels in blood.
3. Adjustment of water content in blood.

The Kidneys

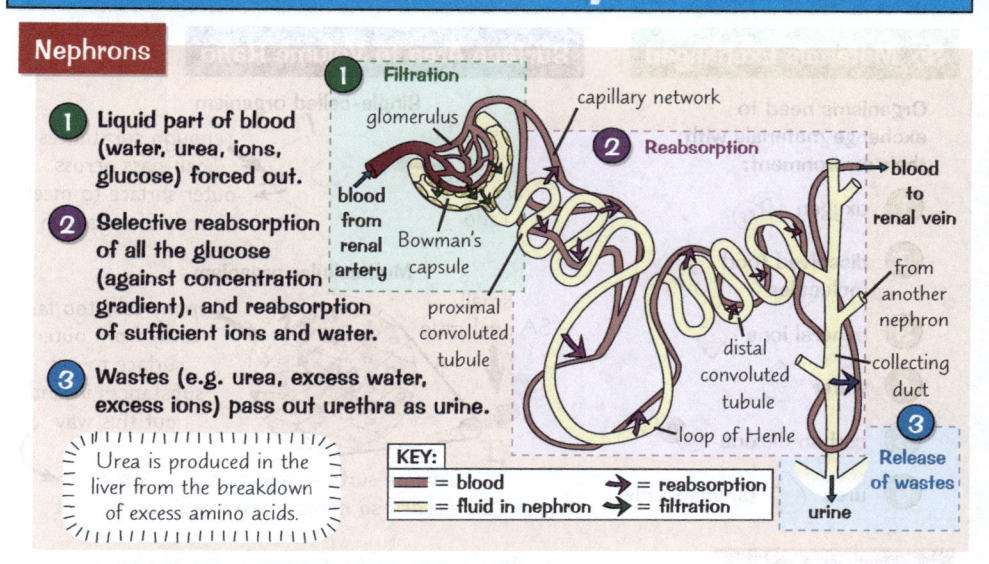

Nephrons

1. Liquid part of blood (water, urea, ions, glucose) forced out.
2. Selective reabsorption of all the glucose (against concentration gradient), and reabsorption of sufficient ions and water.
3. Wastes (e.g. urea, excess water, excess ions) pass out urethra as urine.

Urea is produced in the liver from the breakdown of excess amino acids.

1 Filtration — glomerulus, capillary network, blood from renal artery, Bowman's capsule, proximal convoluted tubule

2 Reabsorption — distal convoluted tubule, loop of Henle, blood to renal vein, from another nephron, collecting duct

3 Release of wastes — urine

KEY:
- ▬ = blood
- ▬ = fluid in nephron
- → = reabsorption
- → = filtration

Controlling the Water Content of the Blood

The water content of the blood is controlled by **anti-diuretic hormone (ADH)**. It makes the collecting ducts of the nephrons more permeable.

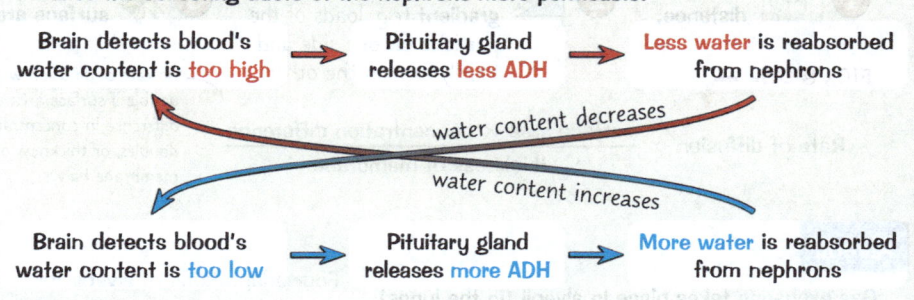

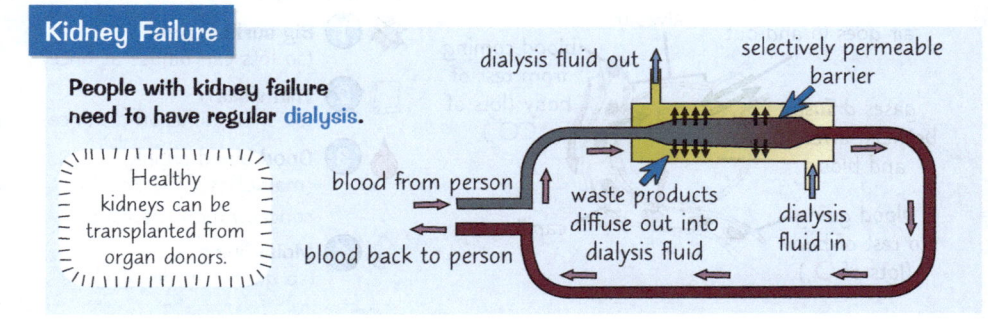

Brain detects blood's water content is **too high** → Pituitary gland releases **less ADH** → **Less water** is reabsorbed from nephrons

water content decreases

water content increases

Brain detects blood's water content is **too low** → Pituitary gland releases **more ADH** → **More water** is reabsorbed from nephrons

Kidney Failure

People with kidney failure need to have regular **dialysis**.

Healthy kidneys can be transplanted from organ donors.

dialysis fluid out, selectively permeable barrier, blood from person, waste products diffuse out into dialysis fluid, dialysis fluid in, blood back to person

Topic 7 — Animal Coordination, Control & Homeostasis

Topic 8 — Exchange and Transport in Animals

Exchange of Materials

Six Materials Exchanged

Organisms need to exchange materials with their environment:

1. oxygen
2. dissolved food molecules
3. mineral ions
4. water
5. carbon dioxide
6. urea (animals only)

Surface Area to Volume Ratio

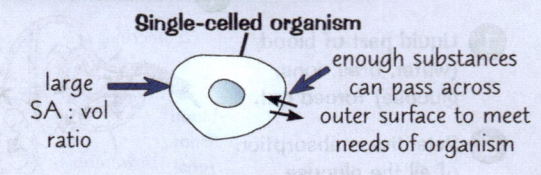

Single-celled organism — large SA : vol ratio — enough substances can pass across outer surface to meet needs of organism

Multicellular organism — small SA : vol ratio — many cells too far away from outer surface to get substances in and out this way

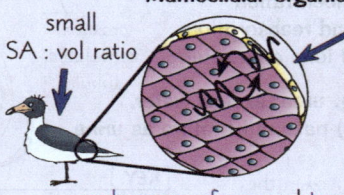

exchange surfaces and transport systems are needed so needs of every cell can be met

Rate of Diffusion

These three factors increase the rate of diffusion:

1. A short distance.
2. A high concentration gradient (e.g. loads of the particles on one side and hardly any on the other).
3. A large surface area.

FICK'S LAW

$$\text{Rate of diffusion} \propto \frac{\text{surface area} \times \text{concentration difference}}{\text{thickness of membrane}}$$

So rate of diffusion will double if surface area or difference in concentration doubles, or thickness of membrane halves.

Alveoli

Gas exchange takes place in alveoli (in the lungs).

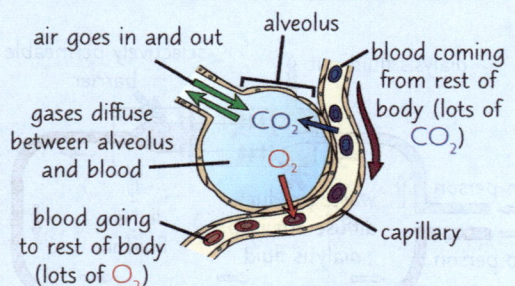

- air goes in and out
- alveolus
- gases diffuse between alveolus and blood
- blood coming from rest of body (lots of CO_2)
- blood going to rest of body (lots of O_2)
- capillary

Four adaptations of alveoli for gas exchange:

1. **Big surface area** (so lots can diffuse at once)
2. **Thin walls** (so short diffusion distance)
3. **Good blood supply** (maintains CO_2 and O_2 concentration gradients)
4. **Moist lining** (so gases can dissolve)

Blood and Blood Vessels

Four Blood Components

Component	Function	Description
1 Red blood cells (erythrocytes)	Carry oxygen around the body.	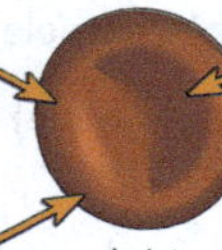 no nucleus so more room for O_2; biconcave shape = big surface area = lots of O_2 absorbed; contains haemoglobin, which binds to O_2
2 White blood cells	Defend against infection.	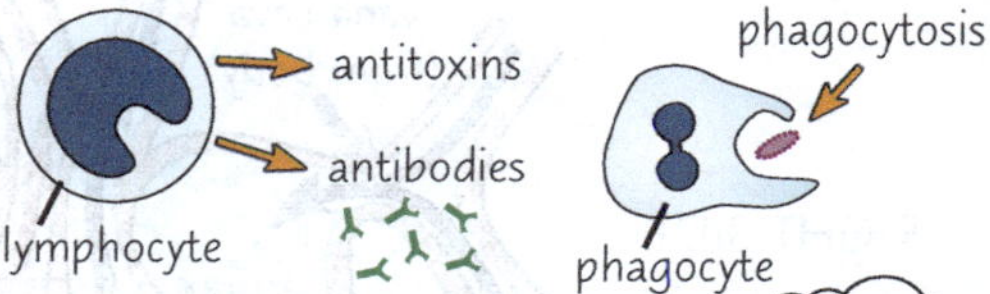 lymphocyte → antitoxins, antibodies; phagocyte → phagocytosis
3 Platelets	Help blood to clot at a wound.	 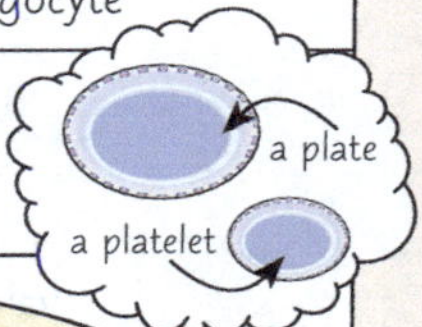 fragments of cells; a plate / a platelet
4 Plasma	Carries everything in the blood.	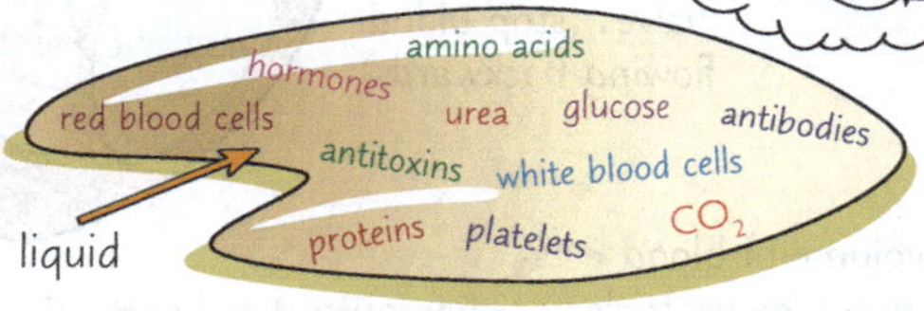 liquid; red blood cells, hormones, amino acids, urea, glucose, antibodies, antitoxins, white blood cells, proteins, platelets, CO_2

Three Types of Blood Vessel

1 Arteries carry blood away from the heart.
lumen
thick muscle and elastic layers because blood pressure is high

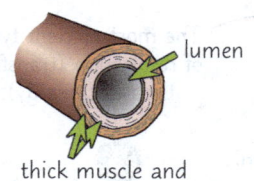

2 Capillaries carry blood close to body cells to exchange substances.
thin, permeable walls to allow substances to diffuse in and out easily

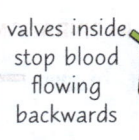

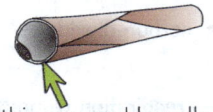

3 Veins carry blood back to the heart.
valves inside stop blood flowing backwards
thinner walls than arteries because blood pressure is lower

Topic 8 — Exchange and Transport in Animals

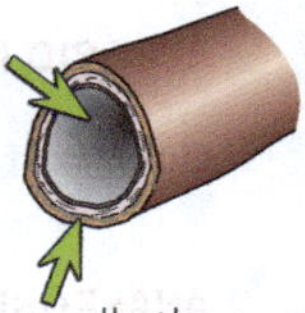

The Heart and Respiration

The Heart

The circulatory system is made up of the heart, blood vessels and blood.
Humans have a double circulatory system (two circuits):

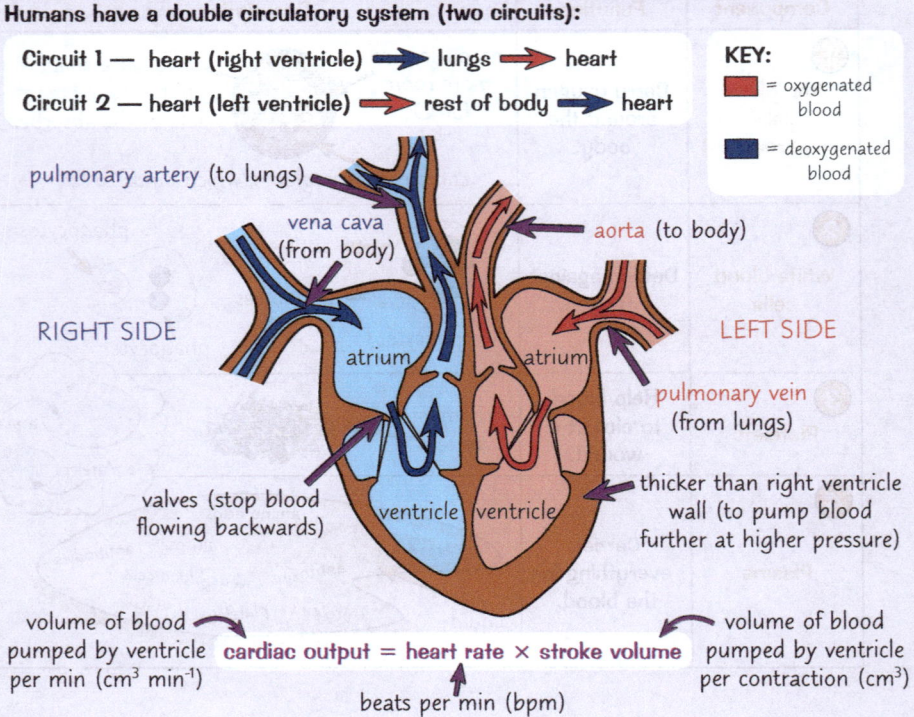

Circuit 1 — heart (right ventricle) → lungs → heart
Circuit 2 — heart (left ventricle) → rest of body → heart

KEY:
- = oxygenated blood
- = deoxygenated blood

- pulmonary artery (to lungs)
- vena cava (from body)
- aorta (to body)
- RIGHT SIDE
- atrium / atrium
- LEFT SIDE
- pulmonary vein (from lungs)
- valves (stop blood flowing backwards)
- ventricle / ventricle
- thicker than right ventricle wall (to pump blood further at higher pressure)

volume of blood pumped by ventricle per min ($cm^3\ min^{-1}$) ← **cardiac output = heart rate × stroke volume** → volume of blood pumped by ventricle per contraction (cm^3)

beats per min (bpm)

Respiration

RESPIRATION — the process of transferring energy from glucose.
It's an exothermic reaction that goes on continuously in living cells.
The energy transferred is used for metabolic processes.

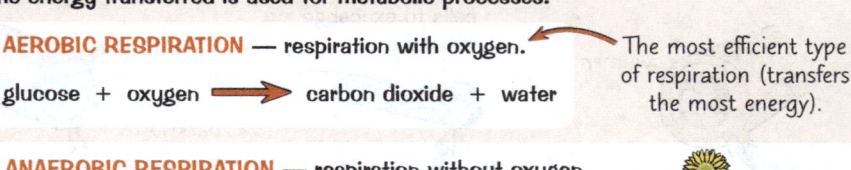

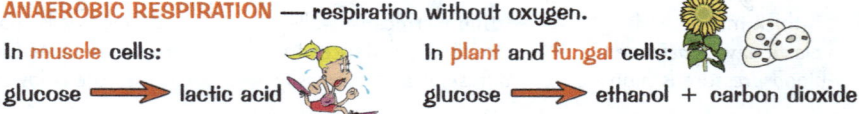

AEROBIC RESPIRATION — respiration with oxygen. ← The most efficient type of respiration (transfers the most energy).

glucose + oxygen → carbon dioxide + water

ANAEROBIC RESPIRATION — respiration without oxygen.

In muscle cells:

glucose → lactic acid

In plant and fungal cells:

glucose → ethanol + carbon dioxide

Topic 8 — Exchange and Transport in Animals

Topic 9 — Ecosystems and Material Cycles

Ecosystems and Organism Interactions

Levels of Organisation

Habitat — the place where an organism lives.

INDIVIDUAL	A single organism.
POPULATION	All the organisms of one species in a habitat.
COMMUNITY	The populations of different species living in a habitat.
ECOSYSTEM	A community of organisms along with all the non-living conditions.

Interdependence

INTERDEPENDENCE — each species in a community depending upon other species for things, e.g. food or shelter.

So a change in the population of one species can affect other species in the same community.

Two types of relationship between organisms:

1 MUTUALISM — Both organisms benefit.

2 PARASITISM — Parasite lives in or on host. Parasite benefits but the host doesn't.

Factors Affecting Communities

Both biotic (living) and abiotic (non-living) factors can affect organisms in a community:

- Light intensity
- Amount of water
- Competition
- Temperature
- Levels of pollutants
- Predation

number of predators increases → number of prey decreases
↑ ↓
number of prey increases ← number of predators decreases

Biomass and Energy Transfers

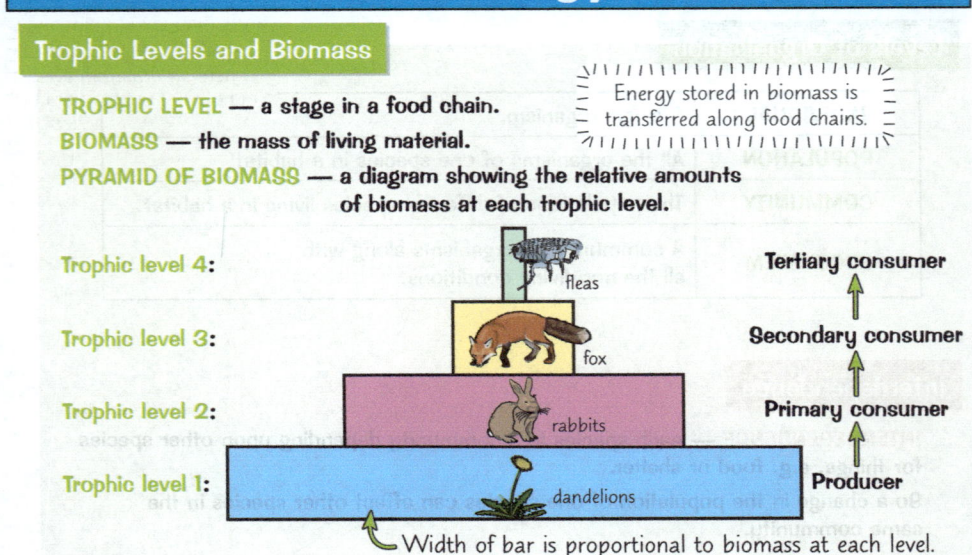

Trophic Levels and Biomass

TROPHIC LEVEL — a stage in a food chain.
BIOMASS — the mass of living material.
PYRAMID OF BIOMASS — a diagram showing the relative amounts of biomass at each trophic level.

Energy stored in biomass is transferred along food chains.

- Trophic level 4: fleas — Tertiary consumer
- Trophic level 3: fox — Secondary consumer
- Trophic level 2: rabbits — Primary consumer
- Trophic level 1: dandelions — Producer

Width of bar is proportional to biomass at each level.

Energy Transfer

Energy from the Sun is transferred by light to producers.

A small % of energy that hits producers is converted into glucose and stored as biomass.

Only some energy available at one trophic level is passed on to the next.

Here are three reasons why energy is **lost** between trophic levels:

1. Not all of the material ingested by an organism is absorbed, some is lost as faeces.
2. Some energy is transferred from organisms to the surroundings as heat.
3. Lots of energy is used for respiration rather than being used to build new biomass.

Three impacts of energy loss:
1. Fewer organisms at each trophic level
2. Gives triangular shape to pyramid of biomass
3. Rarely more than five trophic levels in a food chain

$$\text{efficiency of energy transfer (\%)} = \frac{\text{energy transferred to the next level}}{\text{energy available at the previous level}} \times 100$$

'Energy' can be swapped for 'biomass'.

Topic 9 — Ecosystems and Material Cycles

Human Impacts on Biodiversity

Eutrophication

BIODIVERSITY — the variety of living organisms in an ecosystem.

EUTROPHICATION — a process in which an excess of nutrients builds up in water, which can lead to a reduction in biodiversity:

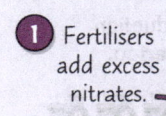

1. Fertilisers add excess nitrates.
2. Excess nitrates cause algae to grow fast and block out light.
3. Plants can't photosynthesise — they die and decompose.
4. Microorganisms that eat decomposing plants multiply and use up oxygen.
5. Organisms that need oxygen die.

Fish Farms

Four ways fish farming can reduce biodiversity:

1. Waste and food from the nets can enter open water and cause eutrophication.
2. Parasites can escape from the farm and infect wild animals (which can kill them).
3. Predators can be trapped in the nets and die.
4. Farmed fish can escape and compete with wild populations (e.g. for food).

Non-Indigenous Species

Non-indigenous species don't naturally occur in an area.

They can cause native species to die out because:

- they can out-compete native species.
- they can bring new diseases to a habitat.

Maintaining Biodiversity

Two ways of improving biodiversity:

1. **Reforestation** (replanting trees where they've been removed)

Forests generally have high biodiversity as they contain a wide variety of plants, which support lots of animal species.

2. **Conservation schemes** — for example:
- protecting species' natural habitat,
- protecting species in safe areas (e.g. zoos),
- breeding organisms to increase population.

Five benefits of maintaining biodiversity on global and local scales:

1. Preserves cultural heritage.
2. Ensures there's enough food for future generations.
3. Saves potential future medicines.
4. Creates jobs.
5. Brings money to areas through ecotourism.

Topic 9 — Ecosystems and Material Cycles

Food Security

Increasing Population

FOOD SECURITY — having enough food to feed a population that is accessible, safe to eat, and has the right balance of nutrition.

Population growth affects food security:

Global population is increasing... → ...so food production must increase too.

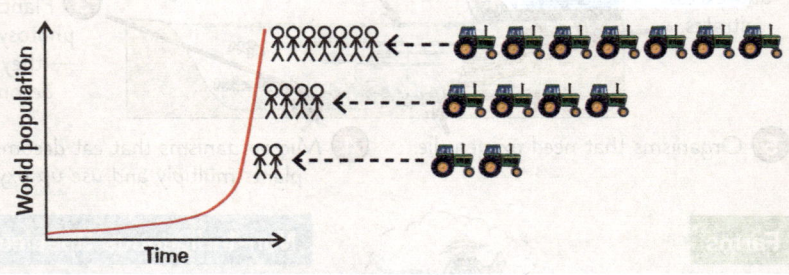

Four More Factors Affecting Food Security

1) Changing diets (increased consumption of meat and fish)

- For a given area of land, less food can be produced from animals than can be produced from crops.
- Animals are often fed crops, meaning there are fewer crops available for humans.

2) Environmental changes caused by human activity

- Burning fossil fuels releases CO_2 — this leads to climate change, which can reduce crop yields.
- Soil pollution can reduce crop growth.

3) New pests and pathogens

Crops and livestock can be damaged so less can become food for humans.

4) Sustainability

- Some crops are grown to make **biofuels** (renewable alternatives to fossil fuels). This may need to be limited in the future so the land can be used for food crops instead.
- High input costs of farming may mean some areas will not be farmed in the future — which may reduce food production.

Sustainable methods of food production are needed to feed everyone now and in the future.

Topic 9 — Ecosystems and Material Cycles

Cycling of Materials

Recycling Materials

Materials are cycled through the abiotic and biotic parts of an ecosystem.

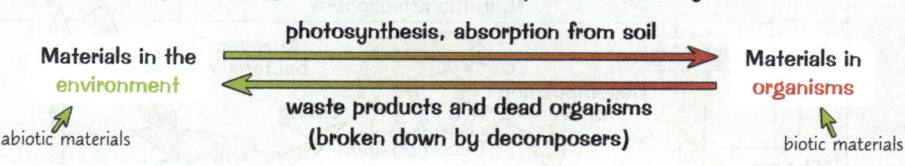

Materials in the **environment** (abiotic materials) → photosynthesis, absorption from soil → Materials in **organisms** (biotic materials)

Materials in organisms → waste products and dead organisms (broken down by decomposers) → Materials in the environment

The Water Cycle

POTABLE WATER — water that's drinkable.

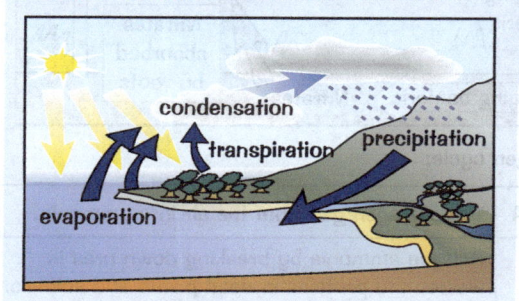

Water cycle diagram showing: evaporation, condensation, transpiration, precipitation.

In times of drought, potable water can be produced from salt water by **desalination**:

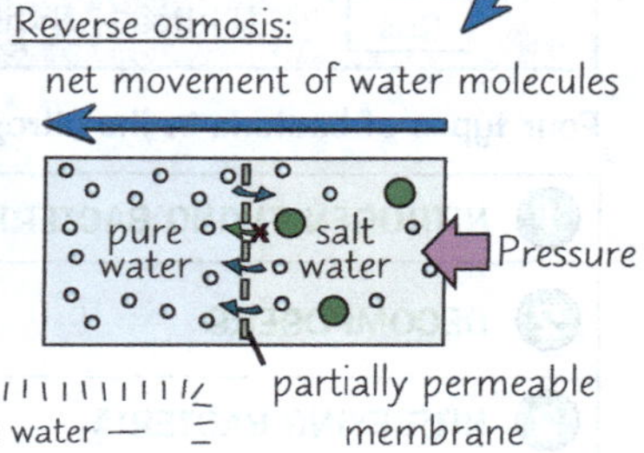

Reverse osmosis: net movement of water molecules

Diagram showing pure water and salt water separated by a partially permeable membrane, with Pressure applied.

Thermal desalination can also be used to get pure water — salt water is boiled then the steam is condensed and collected.

The Carbon Cycle

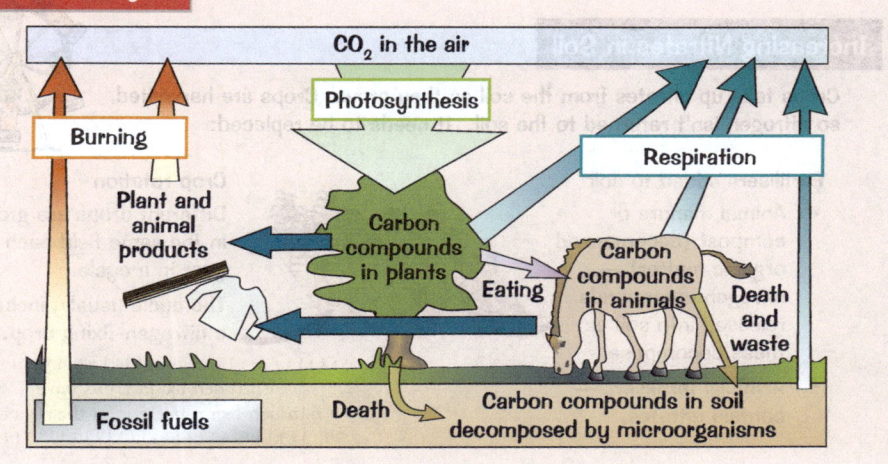

CO_2 in the air

- Photosynthesis → Carbon compounds in plants
- Respiration ← from plants and animals
- Burning → CO_2 in the air
- Plant and animal products
- Eating: Carbon compounds in plants → Carbon compounds in animals
- Death and waste → Carbon compounds in soil decomposed by microorganisms
- Death → Fossil fuels

Topic 9 — Ecosystems and Material Cycles

Nitrogen

The Nitrogen Cycle

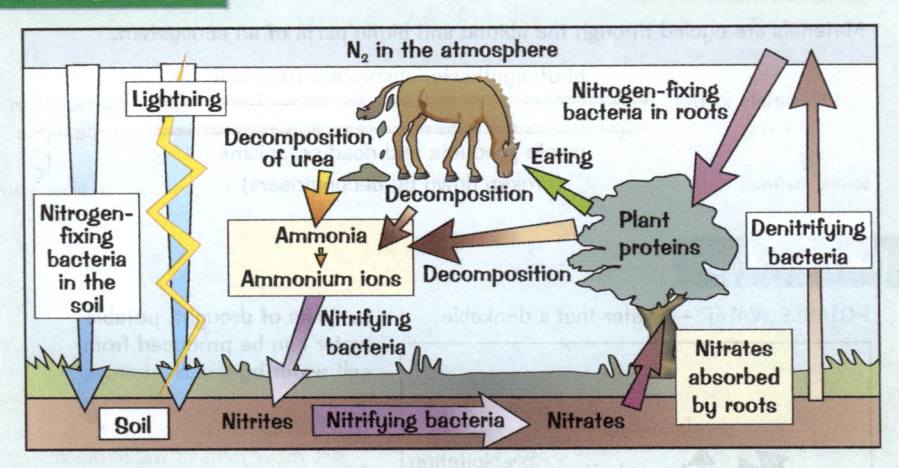

Four types of bacteria in the nitrogen cycle:

①	**NITROGEN-FIXING BACTERIA**	Turn nitrogen gas from the air into ammonia.
②	**DECOMPOSERS**	Release ammonia by breaking down urea in waste, and proteins in dead plants and animals.
③	**NITRIFYING BACTERIA**	Turn ammonia into nitrites, then into nitrates.
④	**DENITRIFYING BACTERIA**	Turn nitrates into nitrogen gas.

Increasing Nitrates in Soil

Crops take up nitrates from the soil as they grow. Crops are harvested, so nitrogen isn't returned to the soil. It needs to be replaced:

Fertilisers added to soil
- Animal manure or compost (decomposed organic matter) — nitrogen compounds released into soil as these decompose.
- Artificial fertilisers — contain nitrates.

Crop rotation

Different crops are grown in the same field each year in a cycle.

The cycle usually includes a nitrogen-fixing crop.

Nitrogen-fixing crops have nitrogen-fixing bacteria in their roots.

Topic 9 — Ecosystems and Material Cycles

Indicator Species and Decomposition

Indicator Species

INDICATOR SPECIES — organisms that are very sensitive to changes in their environment and so can be used to investigate pollution.

Two methods to investigate pollution using indicator species:

	Organisms present when low pollution	Organisms present when high pollution
Water	• stonefly larvae • freshwater shrimp	• blood worms • sludgeworms
Air	• bushy lichen • blackspot fungus (on rose leaves)	• crusty lichen (or no lichen)

1 Do a survey to see if species is present or absent. Quick but doesn't show how polluted area is.

2 Count the number of times the species occurs in an area. Allows you to compare areas.

Using indicator species is easy and cost-effective, but isn't accurate — factors other than pollution can affect their numbers.

Three Things that Increase Decomposition Rate

1 Warm temperature — speeds up enzyme-controlled reactions in decomposers.

2 Moist conditions — decomposers need water to survive.

3 Plenty of oxygen — decomposers need oxygen for aerobic respiration.

$$\text{rate of decomposition} = \frac{\text{amount of decomposition}}{\text{time}}$$

Can be measured in different ways, e.g. the amount of decomposer present.

Making Compost

Decomposition rate increased by:

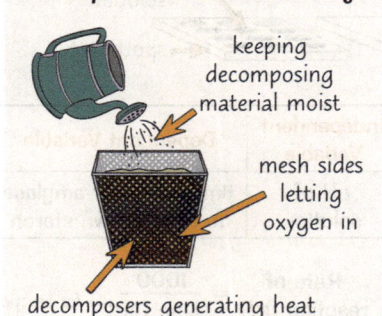

- keeping decomposing material moist
- mesh sides letting oxygen in
- decomposers generating heat

Three Methods of Food Preservation

Decomposition rate decreased by:

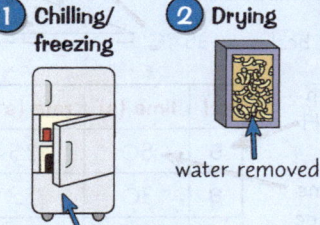

1 Chilling/freezing — low temperature (so growth rate of decomposers slowed/stopped)

2 Drying — water removed

3 Canning — airtight (so no oxygen available), sterilised to kill decomposers

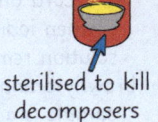

Topic 9 — Ecosystems and Material Cycles

Core Practicals 1

Microscopy

Start with the lowest-powered lens then move the stage up with the coarse adjustment knob.

↓

Look down the eyepiece and adjust the focus with the adjustment knobs (use the coarse one first).

↓

To see the slide with a greater magnification, swap to a higher-powered lens and refocus.

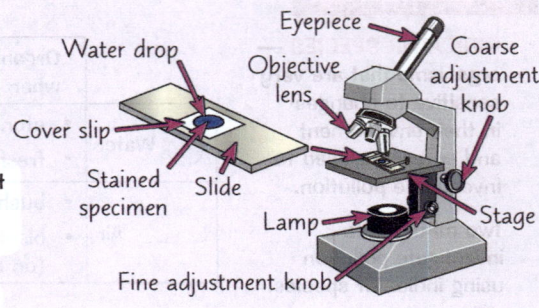

Labels on microscope diagram: Water drop, Cover slip, Stained specimen, Slide, Eyepiece, Objective lens, Coarse adjustment knob, Lamp, Stage, Fine adjustment knob

$$\text{total magnification} = \text{eyepiece lens magnification} \times \text{objective lens magnification}$$

Drawing your observations:
- use a sharp pencil
- draw unbroken lines
- label important features
- include a magnification scale.

Plant Cell, × 400 — nucleus, chloroplasts, cell wall — 0.1 mm

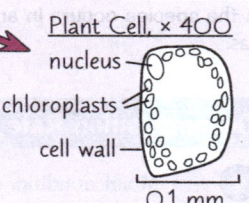

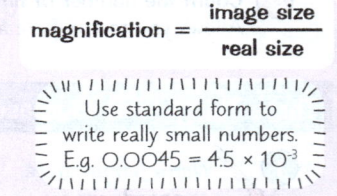

$$\text{magnification} = \frac{\text{image size}}{\text{real size}}$$

Use standard form to write really small numbers. E.g. $0.0045 = 4.5 \times 10^{-3}$

Effect of pH on Amylase Activity

check regularly and adjust heat to keep temperature constant

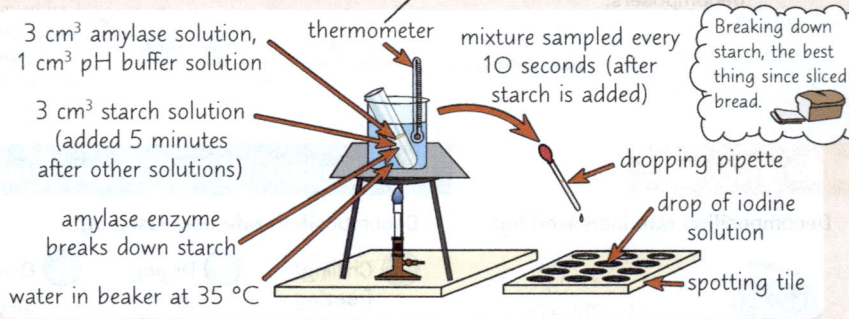

- $3\ cm^3$ amylase solution, $1\ cm^3$ pH buffer solution
- thermometer
- $3\ cm^3$ starch solution (added 5 minutes after other solutions)
- amylase enzyme breaks down starch
- water in beaker at 35 °C
- mixture sampled every 10 seconds (after starch is added)
- dropping pipette
- drop of iodine solution
- spotting tile

Breaking down starch, the best thing since sliced bread.

repeat with different pH buffers

record time when iodine solution remains browny-orange after sample is added

pH	time (s)	rate (s⁻¹)
5	80	12.5
6	30	33.3
7	50	20.0
8	90	11.1

Independent Variable	Dependent Variable
pH of solution	time taken for amylase to break down starch

$$\text{Rate of reaction (s}^{-1}) = \frac{1000}{\text{time (s)}} \text{ for reaction to happen}$$

Core Practicals 2

Testing for Biological Molecules

Test	Method	Positive result
Benedict's test (for reducing sugars)	Add Benedict's reagent to a food sample and leave in a water bath at 75 °C.	blue → green / yellow / brick red
Iodine test (for starch)	Add iodine solution to a food sample and mix.	browny-orange → blue-black
Biuret test (for proteins)	Add potassium hydroxide solution to a food sample, followed by some copper(II) sulfate solution.	blue → purple
Emulsion test (for lipids)	Add ethanol to a food sample and shake for a minute. Pour the solution into water.	milky emulsion

Osmosis

Four steps to investigate osmosis in potatoes:

1. Cut a potato into identical cylinders.
2. Divide the cylinders into groups of three and measure the mass of each group.
3. Prepare beakers containing different concentrations of sucrose solution and one of pure water. Put one group of cylinders in each beaker.
4. Leave for at least 40 minutes, then take out the cylinders and dry them gently with a paper towel. Measure the mass of each group again.

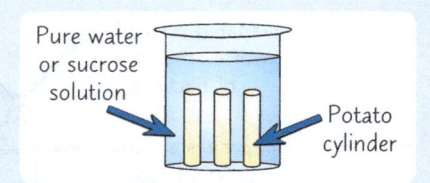

$$\% \text{ change in mass} = \frac{\text{final mass} - \text{initial mass}}{\text{initial mass}} \times 100$$

Independent Variable	Dependent Variable
concentration of sucrose solution	potato cylinder mass

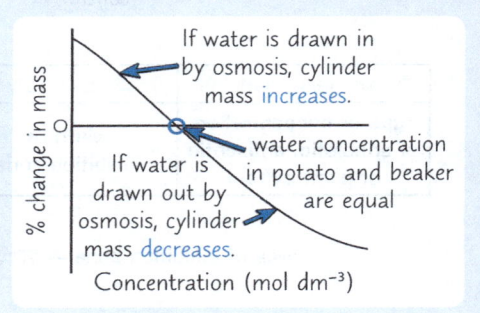

If water is drawn in by osmosis, cylinder mass increases.

If water is drawn out by osmosis, cylinder mass decreases.

water concentration in potato and beaker are equal

Concentration (mol dm^{-3})

Core Practicals

Core Practicals 3

Antibiotics and Antiseptics

Five steps to prepare an *aseptic culture* of bacteria in a lab:

1. A Petri dish and some agar jelly are sterilised in an autoclave to kill any unwanted microorganisms in them.

2. Hot agar jelly is poured into the Petri dish and allowed to cool and set.

3. An inoculating loop is passed through a hot flame to sterilise it.

4. The inoculating loop is used to transfer bacteria to the agar jelly.

5. The Petri dish is lightly taped shut to stop microorganisms in the air getting in. It is stored at 25 °C and upside down to stop drops of condensation falling on the agar surface.

Bacteria can also be grown in a nutrient broth solution. This is sterilised before use and kept covered whenever possible to prevent unwanted microorganisms entering.

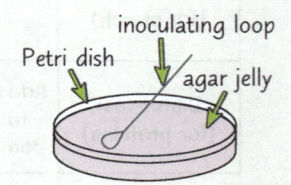

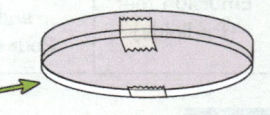

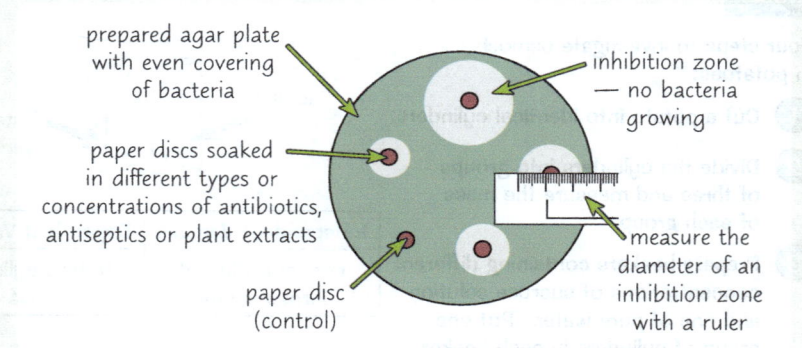

Labels: inoculating loop, Petri dish, agar jelly

Labels on agar plate diagram:
- prepared agar plate with even covering of bacteria
- inhibition zone — no bacteria growing
- paper discs soaked in different types or concentrations of antibiotics, antiseptics or plant extracts
- paper disc (control)
- measure the diameter of an inhibition zone with a ruler

Independent Variable	Dependent Variable
type or concentration of antibiotic, antiseptic or plant extract	width of inhibition zone

More effective antibiotic/ antiseptic/ plant extract ⟶ Wider inhibition zone

area of inhibition zone = πr^2 — r is the radius (half the diameter)

Core Practicals 4

Effect of Light Intensity on Photosynthesis Rate

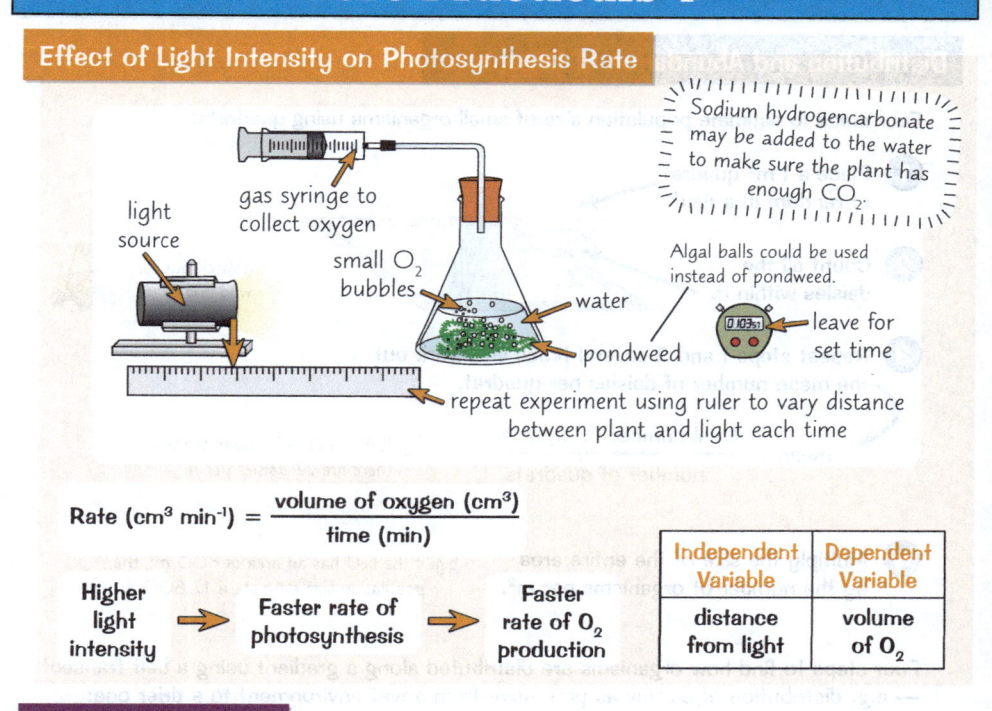

Sodium hydrogencarbonate may be added to the water to make sure the plant has enough CO_2.

- light source
- gas syringe to collect oxygen
- small O_2 bubbles
- water
- pondweed
- Algal balls could be used instead of pondweed.
- leave for set time
- repeat experiment using ruler to vary distance between plant and light each time

$$\text{Rate (cm}^3\text{ min}^{-1}) = \frac{\text{volume of oxygen (cm}^3)}{\text{time (min)}}$$

Higher light intensity → Faster rate of photosynthesis → Faster rate of O_2 production

Independent Variable	Dependent Variable
distance from light	volume of O_2

Rate of Respiration

A respirometer can be used to investigate the effect of temperature on respiration rate:

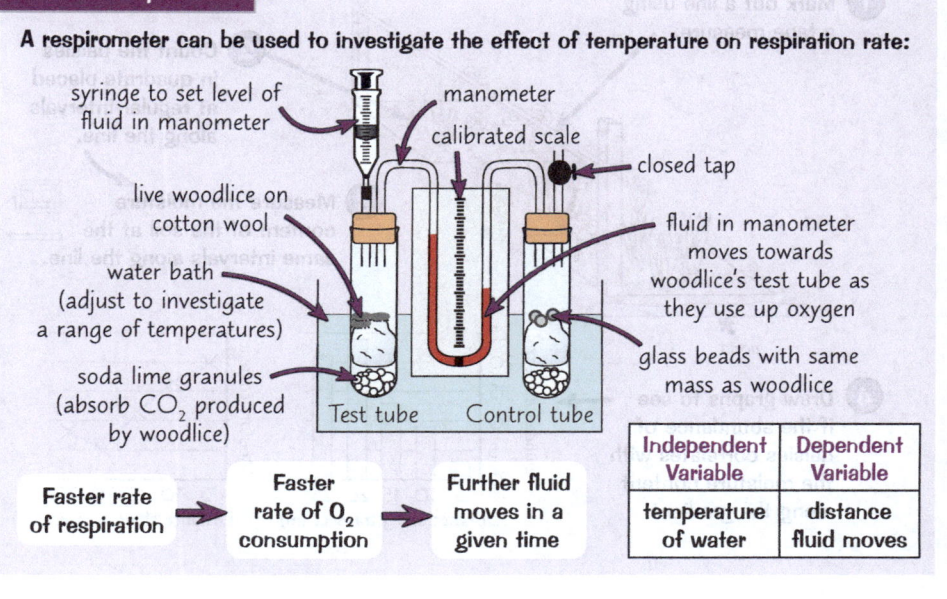

- syringe to set level of fluid in manometer
- manometer
- calibrated scale
- closed tap
- live woodlice on cotton wool
- fluid in manometer moves towards woodlice's test tube as they use up oxygen
- water bath (adjust to investigate a range of temperatures)
- soda lime granules (absorb CO_2 produced by woodlice)
- glass beads with same mass as woodlice
- Test tube
- Control tube

Faster rate of respiration → Faster rate of O_2 consumption → Further fluid moves in a given time

Independent Variable	Dependent Variable
temperature of water	distance fluid moves

Core Practicals 5

Distribution and Abundance of Organisms

Four steps to estimate population size of small organisms using quadrats:

1. Place a 1 m² quadrat at random in a field.
2. Count all the daisies within it.

   Watch out for wild quad-rats.

3. Repeat steps 1 and 2 several times and work out the mean number of daisies per quadrat.

   $$\text{mean} = \frac{\text{total number of organisms}}{\text{number of quadrats}}$$

   E.g. 154 daisies in 7 quadrats means there are 22 daisies per m².

4. Multiply the size of the entire area by the number of organisms per m².

   E.g. if the field has an area of 800 m², the population size estimate is 17 600 daisies.

Four steps to find how organisms are distributed along a gradient using a belt transect — e.g. distribution of daisies as you move from a wet environment to a drier one:

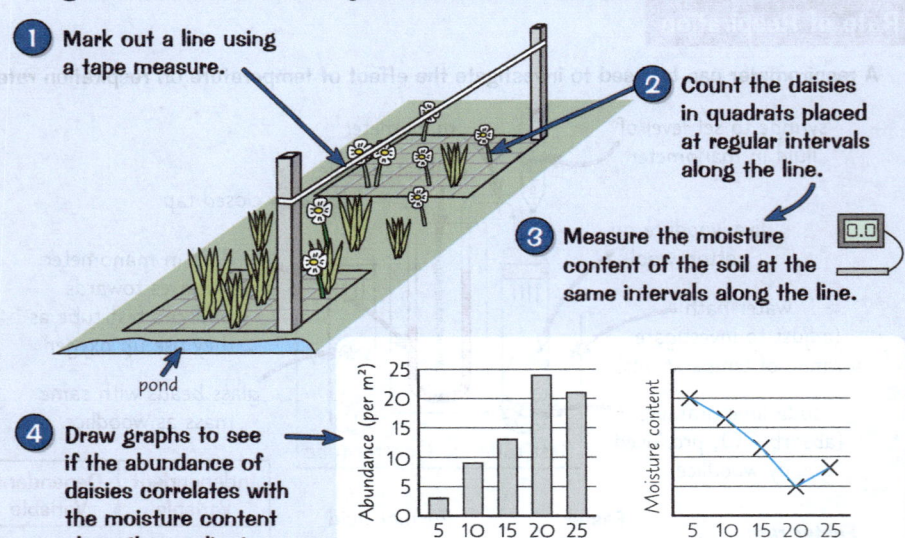

1. Mark out a line using a tape measure.
2. Count the daisies in quadrats placed at regular intervals along the line.
3. Measure the moisture content of the soil at the same intervals along the line.
4. Draw graphs to see if the abundance of daisies correlates with the moisture content along the gradient.

Practical Techniques

Heating

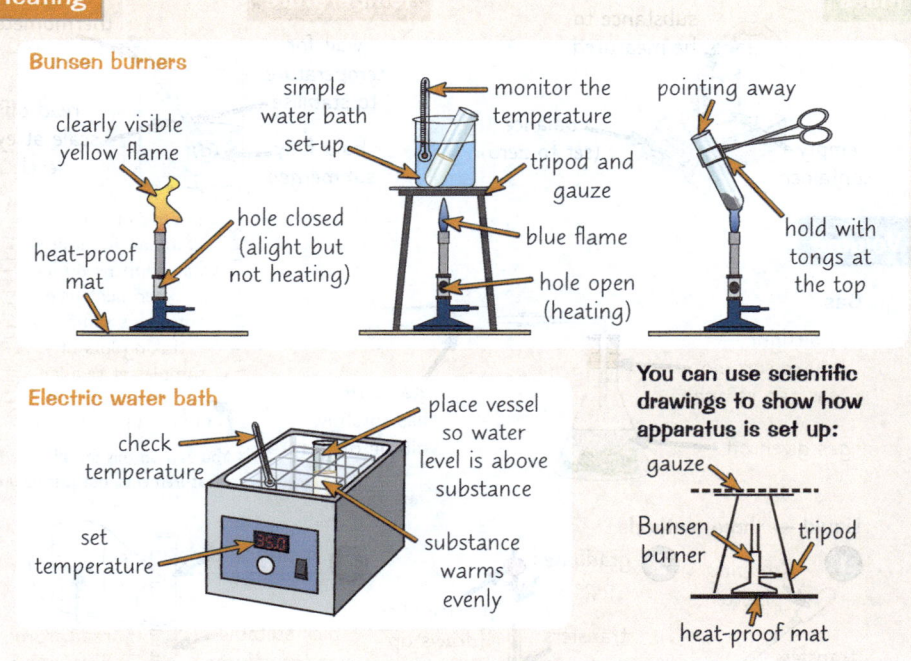

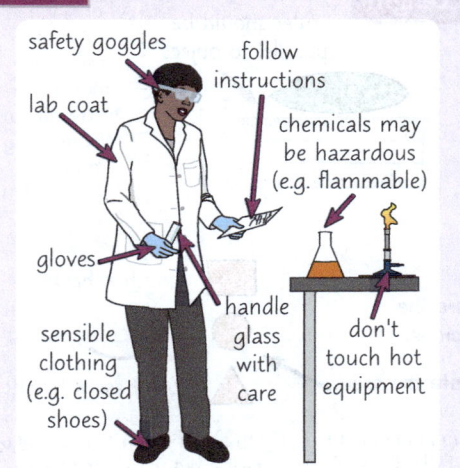

Bunsen burners

- clearly visible yellow flame
- heat-proof mat
- simple water bath set-up
- hole closed (alight but not heating)
- monitor the temperature
- tripod and gauze
- blue flame
- hole open (heating)
- pointing away
- hold with tongs at the top

Electric water bath

- check temperature
- set temperature
- place vessel so water level is above substance
- substance warms evenly

You can use scientific drawings to show how apparatus is set up:
- gauze
- Bunsen burner
- tripod
- heat-proof mat

Safety

- safety goggles
- lab coat
- gloves
- sensible clothing (e.g. closed shoes)
- follow instructions
- chemicals may be hazardous (e.g. flammable)
- handle glass with care
- don't touch hot equipment

Ethics

Any organisms used in an investigation need to be treated safely and ethically.

- Animals kept in the lab should be cared for in a humane way.
- Wild animals captured for study should be returned to their original habitat.

Other students shouldn't be forced or pressured into participating in experiments.

Measurements

Mass
- substance to be measured
- empty container
- balance (set to zero)

Temperature
- wait for temperature to stabilise
- bulb fully submerged
- thermometer
- read off scale at eye level

Volume

Gas
- airtight — make sure no gas can escape
- gas given off
- gas syringe fills to show volume of gas

You can monitor what happens during an experiment using **continuous sampling** (taking lots of samples at regular intervals).

You can do this for all measurements, not just volume.

Liquid — three methods
1. **dropping pipette** — transfers drops
2. **graduated pipette** — transfers accurate volumes; pipette filler (draws up liquid)
3. **measuring cylinder** — pick suitable size for volume required; read from bottom of meniscus

Time
- stopwatch
- stopwatches are sensitive
- start and stop the timer at the exact right time

Length
- ruler should be parallel to object
- You can use a tape measure or metre rule to measure long distances.

pH
- Indicator dyes
- Indicator paper
- pH meters

Area
1. Measure the dimensions.
2. Calculate the area.

- ▇ length × height
- ● πr^2 (r = radius)
- ▲ ½ × base × height

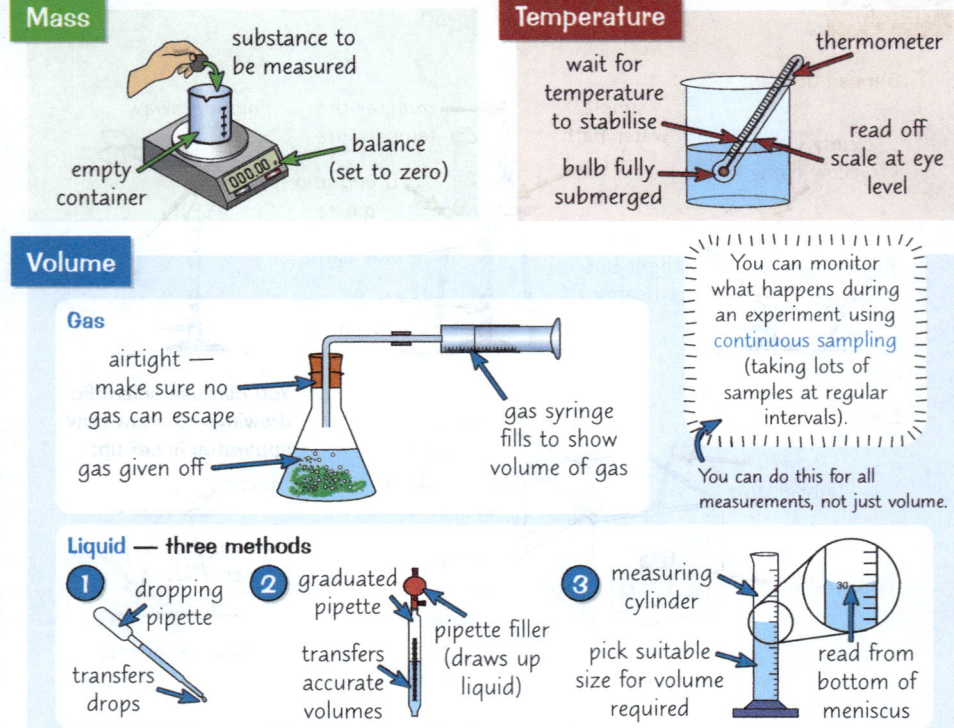

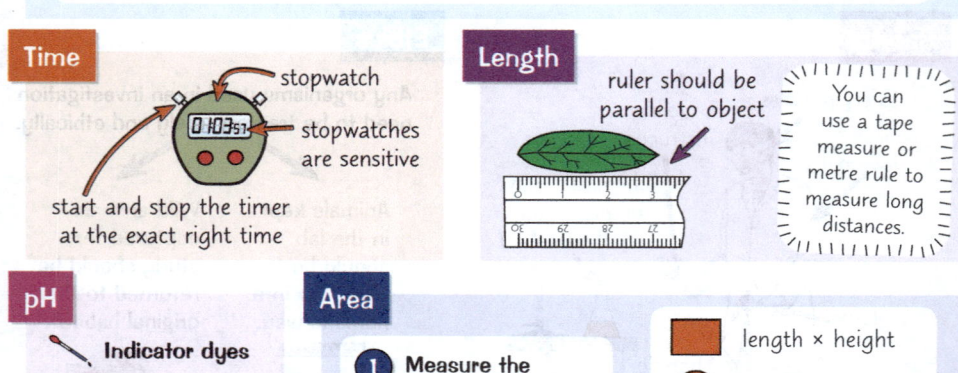

Hooray! You did it — you got through ALL the facts. Give yourself a big pat on the back.

Practical Skills